ICONS

WEB DESIGN
BEST STUDIOS

Ed. Julius Wiedemann

TASCHEN

KÖLN LONDON LOS ANGELES MADRID PARIS TOKYO

CONTENTS

Web Design: Best Studios

When you surf the web and find a particular website you like, you probably ask yourself who designed it, and how. Brains are the most important assets for making the web dynamic and interesting. The use of the right tools can create the right interface for the right person, product or company. You just have to find the right people that will do the right thing for you, or to serve as the best example for what you need.

This book, in its compact format, displays 90 of the most prominent interactive studios worldwide: web firms that have worked out creative solutions for big and small customers all around the globe. Being an interactive agency doesn't just mean focusing on internet solutions. It has much more to do with the way these professionals think and execute their tasks. When you make work for the web, you have to think differently than when you work for print or film, for example. You may even work for all of them, as some studios indeed do, but working online demands a specific mindset.

The web requires an intensive collaboration of technical and creative resources, where there is still much to be discovered. This ability to work together can produce discoveries that can suddenly become standards for the whole industry. As it is also interactive, innovation allows both programmers and creative professionals to achieve new ways of viewing and envisioning things. The resources available

are plentiful and are changing everyday. A web professional also learns things every day that he or she knows will be useful tomorrow, but soon obsolete. And this ability to be always adaptable can mean the difference between success and failure. Everyone has to work with the idea that the results of the work done are much more measurable than any other medium today. That alone constitutes a profound difference in the approach with the user interacting with the product created. Often, afraid of innovating and making noise, some agencies and professionals tend to be conservative with their online work. What makes these 90 offices special is exactly the opposite. These are professionals committed to both good design and results, and this is essential making the web a better medium every day.

There are certainly many more studios out there with these characteristics, but we had to make what we thought would be a balanced selection. Firstly, we wanted the agencies featured to represent a wide geographical distribution, because solutions are found differently in different cultures. As a result, the 90 companies featured herein are spread out amongst about 30 countries. Secondly, we wanted to incorporate studios and agencies of various sizes. Many times, even interactive agencies that are part of big advertising networks work with very few people. What makes the difference is the quality of the professionals. Thirdly, we researched the portfolios

and clients of those companies, looking at the quality
and innovative aspects of the work. What you will find
is a collection of great solutions to serve as reference
for any person that buys, sells or works on the web.
A visit to the websites mentioned will further enrich
your experience, as the examples included represent
just a small sample of the works listed in their online
portfolios. So we encourage you to visit each studio's
site – we guarantee it will be time well spent.

We have also looked for agencies that have received
awards recently, even though this wasn't the most
important criterion. Awards are mostly granted
after submission, a process that I believe can limit
the spectrum of works reviewed. It is undoubtedly
important to have received awards and it is certainly
a way of measuring results, but we wanted to work
with our own independent selection. We evaluated
more than 3000 offices that do interactive work and
had also to leave out some that we hope to feature in a
future volume.

WEB DESIGN: BEST STUDIOS is the first installment of
a compact book series that highlights the best of the
web. The Web Design titles serve as a reference for the
best ideas, trendsetters, design, navigation concepts,
etc. No matter where the web is involved in your work,
they provide solutions.

Julius Wiedemann

Design Web : les meilleurs studios

Lorsque vous surfez sur le Net, vous vous demandez souvent qui a conçu telle ou telle page et comment. Les méninges sont le meilleur atout pour rendre le Net dynamique et intéressant. Ensuite, utiliser les bons outils permet de créer l'interface idéale pour la personne, le produit ou l'entreprise en question. Il suffit de trouver les professionnels qui vous concocteront ce qui vous convient le mieux ou de servir de meilleur exemple pour ce dont vous avez besoin.

De format compact, cet ouvrage présente 90 des studios interactifs les plus en vue au monde, des entreprises Web qui ont élaboré des solutions créatives pour de petits et gros clients des quatre coins de la planète. Le fait qu'ils soient interactifs ne signifie pas que ces studios se concentrent uniquement sur des solutions en ligne. En effet, ils sont surtout interactifs dans leur manière de penser et d'exécuter les tâches qui leur sont confiées. Lorsque l'on travaille pour le Net, il faut penser différemment que lorsque l'on travaille dans le milieu de l'imprimerie ou du cinéma par exemple. Il est possible d'être actif dans ces domaines, comme le font certains studios, mais le travail en ligne requiert essentiellement une façon de penser spécifique.

Pour commencer, le Net est basé sur une forte synergie de ressources techniques et créatives dont l'exploration est loin d'être terminée. Cette capacité à travailler ensemble peut générer des découvertes qui peuvent soudain devenir la norme pour l'ensemble de la branche. De par son interactivité, l'innovation permet aux programmeurs et aux créatifs de créer de nouvelles manières de visualiser et de visionner les choses. Les ressources disponibles sont énormes et continuent à évoluer chaque jour. Un professionnel du Net est également quelqu'un qui doit apprendre tous les jours des choses dont il sait qu'elles seront utiles demain mais obsolète très vite. Cette capacité à être constamment au goût du jour peut faire la différence entre le succès et l'échec. Il importe de travailler en gardant à l'idée que les résultats sont bien plus mesurables que ceux de tout autre média aujourd'hui. Rien que cela constitue une profonde différence dans l'approche que l'on a avec la personne face à son écran. Bien souvent, par peur d'innover et de créer une onde de choc, beaucoup d'agences et de professionnels ont tendance à se montrer "conservateurs". C'est justement le contraire qui rend le travail de ces 90 agences spécial : ces professionnels sont orientés vers un bon design et vers des résultats, l'une des recettes pour rendre le Net meilleur jour après jour.

Bien d'autres studios présentent certainement ces caractéristiques mais il a bien fallu que nous fassions une sélection pour arriver à un résultat que nous voulions équilibré. Nous souhaitions premièrement obtenir une bonne répartition géographique, les solutions étant considérées différemment selon les cultures. Les 90 studios présentés dans cet ouvrage sont donc répartis dans environ 30 pays. Mais s'agissant du Net, indépendamment de la langue et des aspects culturels, la plupart de ces studios travaillent pour des clients dispersés aux quatre coins du monde ou comptent des entreprises multinationales parmi leurs clients. Les distances géographiques n'ont guère d'importance ici. Deuxièmement, nous voulions intégrer des studios et agences de tailles diverses. Très souvent, même les agences interactives appartenant à de gros réseaux publicitaires travaillent en effectifs très réduits. Ce qui fait alors la différence c'est la compétence des professionnels. Troisièmement, nous avons examiné les références et la clientèle de ces entreprises, en nous concentrant sur la qualité et l'aspect innovant du travail. Le résultat est une collection de formidables solutions auxquelles peut se référer toute personne achetant, vendant ou travaillant sur le Net. Visiter les adresses en ligne est assurément une belle expérience. Les travaux imprimés ne sont qu'un petit échantillon des travaux disponibles dans les références en ligne. N'oubliez donc pas de visiter le site de chaque studio, point de départ d'une nouvelle aventure créative. Vous ne serez pas déçu du voyage.

Nous avons également recherché des agences récemment récompensées, même si cela n'était pas déterminant. Les récompenses sont le plus souvent attribuées après soumission, un processus qui peut limiter l'éventail des travaux examinés. Elles sont indéniablement importantes et constituent certainement une manière de mesurer les résultats, mais nous souhaitions faire notre propre sélection indépendante. Nous avons sûrement passé plus de 3000 agences en revue et avons dû écarter certaines que nous espérons pouvoir présenter dans un prochain tome.

DESIGN WEB : LES MEILLEURS STUDIOS est le premier d'une série d'ouvrages consacrés à montrer le meilleur du Net sous un format compact. Ces publications vous serviront de référence pour trouver les meilleures idées et les meilleurs innovateurs, de superbes design, des concepts de navigation intelligents, etc. Peu importe en quoi le Net affecte votre travail, elles constitueront l'un de vos fournisseurs de solutions. Et si vous n'êtes pas encore sur le Net, elles seront vos meilleurs guides pour un démarrage couronné de succès.

Julius Wiedemann

Web Design: Die besten Studios

Wenn Sie im Web surfen, fragen Sie sich sicher oft, wer hat wohl diese oder jene Seite erstellt und vor allem, wie. Kreatives Denken ist die wichtigste Voraussetzung für die Gestaltung einer dynamischen und interessanten Webseite. Die Anwendung der entsprechenden Werkzeuge kann das geeignete Interface für die dementsprechende Person, ein Produkt oder eine Firma darstellen. Sie müssen nur die richtigen Personen finden, die Ihnen die richtige Lösung bieten oder Ihnen als geeignetes Beispiel dienen können.

Dieses Buch in seiner kompletten Ausführung fasst 90 der weltweit bekanntesten interaktiven Studios zusammen: Internetgesellschaften, die weltweit kreative Lösungen für grosse und kleine Kunden gefunden haben. Eine interaktive Agentur zu sein, bedeutet allerdings nicht nur, sich auf Problemlösungen online zu beschränken. Viel wichtiger ist, wie diese Agenturen denken und wie sie diesen Prozess umzusetzen. Wenn man für das Netz arbeitet, ist es nötig, anders zu denken, als z.B. bei den Printmedien oder in der Filmindustrie. Man kann auch für alle zugleich tätig sein, wie es einige Studios tatsächlich tun, allerdings erfordert die Arbeit online eine ganz spezielle Denkweise.

Um mit den Unterschieden zu beginnen, das Netz ist auf eine intensive Zusammenarbeit von technischen und kreativen Mitteln angewiesen, bei denen es noch viel zu erarbeiten gibt. Diese mögliche Kooperation kann Entdeckungen hervorrufen, die plötzlich zum Standard für die gesamte Industrie werden können. Da der Prozess auch interaktiv ist, können Neuheiten Programmierern und kreativen Mitarbeitern zu erweiterten Denk- und Sichtweisen verhelfen. Die zur Verfügung stehenden Mittel sind riesig und verändern sich täglich. Ein Internetexperte ist ausserdem jemand, der jeden Tag etwas Neues lernen muss, von dem er genau weiss, es wird ihm morgen nützlich und kurz darauf veraltet sein. Genau diese Fähigkeit, immer auf dem aktuellsten Stand zu sein, kann den Erfolg oder die Niederlage ausmachen. Ausserdem muss man sich darüber im Klaren sein, dass das Ergebnis jeder geleisteten Arbeit wesentlich messbarer ist als bei jeglichem anderen Medium heutzutage. Schon das alleine markiert einen grossen Unterschied in der Beziehungsaufnahme zwischen der Person vor dem Bildschirm und derjenigen auf der anderen Seite. Oft ist es beim Kunden die Angst vor Erneuerung und damit Aufsehen zu erregen, was viele Agenturen und Spezialisten wiederum zu konservativem Verhalten online bewegt. Und eben darin unterscheiden sich diese 90 ausgewählten Agenturen - sie verhalten sich genau entgegengesetzt. Sie sind Experten, die sich zu gutem Design und Lösungen verpflichten, eines der Grundlagen dafür, aus dem Netz täglich ein besseres Medium zu machen.

Sicherlich gibt es noch wesentlich mehr Studios mit den gleichen Qualitäten, hier haben wir eine Auswahl getroffen, die uns geeignet erschien. Besonderes Augenmerk haben wir auf eine gute geographische Verteilung gelegt, da Problemstellungen auf unterschiedliche Weise in unterschiedlichen Kulturkreisen angegangen werden. Folglich sind die hier 90 vorgestellten Firmen in über 30 verschiedenen Ländern ansässig. Genau das ist das Web: Unabhängig von sprachlichen und kulturellen Aspekten, arbeiten die meisten Agenturen für internationale Kunden weltweit und weisen multinationale Firmen in ihrem Portfolio vor. Geographische Entfernungen spielen hier keine Rolle mehr. Ausserdem war es unsere Absicht, Studios und Agenturen verschiedener Grössen miteinzubeziehen. Oftmals gibt es interaktive Agenturen, die Teil eines grossen Werbeagentur-Netzwerks sind und nur wenige Mitarbeiter angestellt haben. Den Unterschied macht die Professionalität dieser Mitarbeiter aus. Ausserdem haben wir uns die Portfolios und Kundenstämme dieser 90 Firmen genauestens angeschaut und dabei besonders auf Qualität und kreative Leistung bei ihren Arbeiten geachtet. Möchten Sie nun im Web kaufen, verkaufen oder arbeiten, wir haben für Sie eine Referenz zu jeglicher Art von Problemlösungen erstellt. Der Besuch dieser Online-Adressen ist ganz sicher eine besondere Erfahrung für Sie. Die hier abgedruckten Arbeiten sind nur ein Beispiel der kompletten Werke, die Sie in den Online-Portfolios finden können. So vergessen sie also nicht, jedes Online-Studio zu besuchen und bereiten sie sich jedesmal auf eine kreative Reise vor. Garantiert keine verschenkte Zeit.

Natürlich haben wir auch Agenturen in Betracht gezogen, die in letzter Zeit Auszeichnungen erhalten haben, obwohl das nicht unser Hauptanliegen war. Auszeichnungen werden normalerweise nach streng festgelegten Kriterien verliehen, was in meinen Augen das Spektrum der ausgewählten Arbeiten limitieren kann. Es ist ganz sicher ein möglicher Weg, Leistungen zu bewerten, aber wir ziehen es vor, unsere eigene, unabhängige Wahl zu treffen. Wir haben uns mehr als 3000 interaktive Studios angeschaut und einige auslassen müssen, die wir hoffentlich in der nächsten Ausgabe mitaufnehmen können.

WEB DESIGN: BEST STUDIOS ist das erste Buch einer Serie in kompaktem Format, das das Beste aus dem Web darstellt. Diese Ausgabe wird Ihnen als Referenz nützlich sein, die besten Ideen, Trendsetter, hervorragendes Design, intelligente Navigationssysteme etc. zu finden. Unabhängig davon, welchen Einfluss das Web auf Ihre Arbeit nimmt, hier werden Sie Problemlösungen finden. Sind Sie noch nicht im Web, so kann Ihnen das vorliegende Werk als Richtlinie für einen erfolgreichen Start behilflich sein.

Julius Wiedemann

2ADVANCED
\<USA\>
www.2advanced.com

www.2advanced.com

Concept

Our work Is based on sensory experience, built through combining elements of image, motion, and sound to illicit a strong emotional reaction from the audience. //// Notre travail est basé sur une aventure sensorielle, qui naît de la conjugaison d'images, d'animations et de sons, le but étant de susciter une réaction émotionnelle forte chez le visiteur. //// Unsere Arbeit basiert auf einer Sinneserfahrung, erzeugt durch die Kombination von Bild-, Bewegungs- und Geräuschelementen, eine unerlaubt starke emotionale Reaktion unserer Besucher zu erreichen.

Name 2Advanced Studios

Founded 1999

Team 22 Employees strong. 2 Creative Directors, 2 Art Directors, 5 Flash Designers with html capabilities, 2 html Builders, 1 3D-Designer, 5 Developers, 3 Business Development, and 2 Marketing and Sales.

Tools Macromedia Flash, Adobe After Effects, Cinema 4D, Particle Illusion, Discreet Combustion.

Location

65 Enterprise
Aliso Viejo, CA 92656
USA

Contact

info@2advanced.com

Awards

WebAwards Competition, Summit Creative Awards, American Design Award, FlashintheCan Awards, SXSW Interactive finalists, Macromedia Site of the Day and numerous Site of the Day awards from Favourite Website Awards.

Clients

Ford Motor Company, Nintendo of America, Bacardi, EA Games, KB Homes, Broadcom, J. Walter Thompson, Warner Brothers, Morgan Creek Pictures and LG Electronics, etc.

6D ESTÚDIO

<BRAZIL>

www.6d.com.br

→ Designing new classics. //// Concevoir de nouveaux classiques. //// Design neuer Klassiker.

www.6d.com.br

Name 6D estúdio

Founded 2003

Team 7 Art Directors, and 1 Programmer.

Tools Macromedia Flash, MySQL, html, XML, and php.

Awards **Location**

R. Visconde de Piraja, 547 / 920
CEP: 22410-900 - Ipanema
Rio de Janeiro - RJ
Brazil

Undisclosed

Contact **Clients**

estudio@6d.com.br

Area Objetos, BLAC, Lenny, Cavendish, CBSG, Dom Joao,
Emmanuelle Bernard, Isabela Capeto, Ipanema Design,
Orlando Cani, Rudge, Seu Martin, 1500 productions, etc.

14BITS
<BRAZIL>
www.14bits.com

Concept

14bits allies creativity with a unique understanding of interactive media to build effective projects in a happy working environment. ////
14bits conjugue créativité et connaissance unique des médias interactifs afin de créer des projets efficaces dans un joyeux environnement de travail.
//// 14bits verbindet Kreativität mit einem ganz speziellen Verständnis für interaktive Medien, mit der Absicht, effektive Projekte in einer
positiven Arbeitsatmosphäre zu entwickeln.

www.tesisweb.com.br

HOME
FILMES | FILMS
RÁDIO | RADIO
EQUIPE | TEAM
PRÊMIOS | AWARDS
CONTATO | CONTACT
TESIS WEBDISC

T E S I S

Name
14bits Produções

Founded
2002

Team
1 General Manager, 2 Account Managers, 2 Art Directors,
3 Multimedia Programmers, and 1 System Engineer.

Tools
Macromedia Flash, Macromedia Director, XML, php, paper, graffiti,
ink, 2D and 3D art, and animation tools.

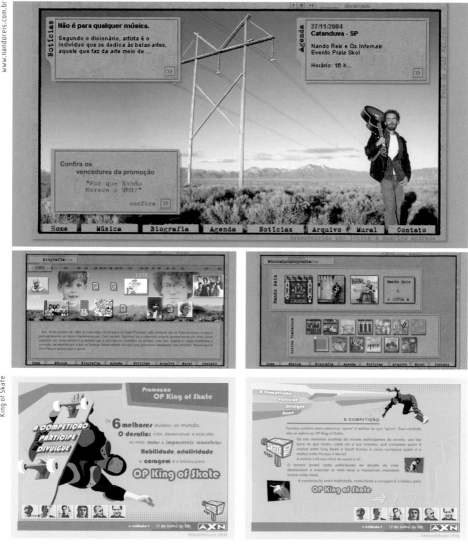

King of Skate

Location

Rua São Benedito, 2522 - 2º andar
Cep: 04735-005 - Alto da Boa Vista
São Paulo - SP
Brazil

Contact

contato@14bits.com.br

Awards

MTV VMB (Best Web Site), Favorite Web Site Awards, New York
Festivals (Silver World Medal), Cannes Cyber Lions (Shortlist),
About Net.Marketing (Gold Medal), Clio Awards (Gold Medal).

Clients

Abbot Laboratories, AOL Brasil, Canal AXN Brasil, Cia Vale do Rio
Doce, General Motors, Leo Burnett, Lobo Filmes, McCann Erickson,
Mc Donald's, MTV Brasil, Pfizer, Sony Entertainment Television,
Sony Pictures International, SOS Mata Atlântica, Telefonica, Tesis,
Unilever, etc.

AGÊNCIACLICK

<BRAZIL>

www.agenciaclick.com.br

Concept

There's nothing more powerfull for a brand than an strategic experience based on a technological breakthrough and wrapped by a compelling idea. //// Rien n'est plus important pour une marque qu'une expérience stratégique basée sur une percée technologique et soutenue par une idée convaincante. //// Es gibt nichts Besseres für ein Produkt, als eine strategische Erfahrung, die auf einem technologischen Durchbruch basiert - das Ganze verpackt in eine zwingendüberzeugende Idee.

www.africa.com.br

Name AgênciaClick

Founded 1992

Team Account Managers, 2 Creative Directors, 7 Art Directors, and 2 Information Architecture Lead.

Tools Adobe Photoshop, html, Macromedia Flash, dhtml, and XML.

Location

Av. Duquesa de Goiás, 716, 2 andar
05686-002 - Real Parque
São Paulo- SP
Brazil

Contact

pcabral@agenciaclick.com.br

Awards

Cannes Lions: Golden/Bronze (various), ONE SHOW Interactive:
Golden/Silver/Bronze Pencil (various), London International
Awards: Gold/Grand Prix (various), Clio Awards: Silver/Bronze
(various), Golden Drum: Gold, Communication Arts Interactive
Design Annual 7: Winner, etc.

Clients

Coca-Cola, Sadia, Fiat, Brastemp, Consul, Bradesco, Caixa Econômica
Federal, Credicard, Diners, GDF - Governo do Distrito Federal,
Gerdau, Açominas, Klabin, MSN, TPI, Emplavi, Grupo Paulo Octavio,
WWF-Brasil, Amil, Comgás, Correios, Net, Sebrae, SENAI, Instituto
Nokia de Tecnologia, Brasil Telecom, Telemig Celular, etc.

AGENCY.COM

<UK/INTERNATIONAL>

www.agency.com

Concept

We create effective interactive marketing campaigns together with world-class websites. Both are important but what's really important is both. Our full service interactive services attract and acquire customers, then sell to and service them in a single coherent digital journey. Advertising agencies create ads. Direct agencies send mail. PR agencies do lunch. We make brands interactive. In an interactive world you need an agency.com. //// Nous créons des campagnes de marketing interactif efficaces et des sites Internet de première catégorie. Les uns et les autres sont importants et interdépendants. L'ensemble de notre gamme de services interactifs permet d'attirer et d'acquérir les clients, puis d'assurer la vente et l'assistance, dans un unique voyage numérique cohérent. Les agences de publicité créent les pubs, les agences de marketing direct se chargent d'envoyer les courriers et les agences de relations publiques s'occupent du déjeuner. Nous rendons les marques interactives. Dans un monde interactif, ce qu'il vous faut est une agency.com. //// Wir lancieren effektive interaktive Marketingkampagnen, zusammen mit Weltklasse-Webseiten. Beides ist wichtig, aber wirklich wichtig ist beides. Unser Komplettpaket für interaktive Dienstleistungen zieht Kunden an, denen wir dann unsere Ideen verkaufen und einen Service in einer einzigen digitalen Reise bieten. Werbeagenturen erstellen Werbung. Versandagenturen verschicken Mailings. PR-Agenturen gehen zum Mittagstisch. Wir kreieren interaktive Produkte. In der interaktiven Welt braucht man eine agency.com.

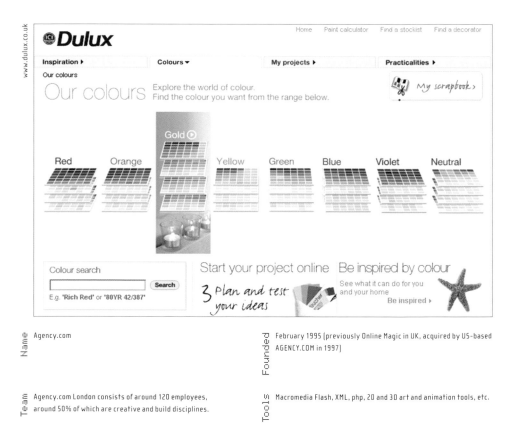

Name
Agency.com

Founded
February 1995 (previously Online Magic in UK, acquired by US-based AGENCY.COM in 1997)

Team
Agency.com London consists of around 120 employees, around 50% of which are creative and build disciplines.

Tools
Macromedia Flash, XML, php, 2D and 3D art and animation tools, etc.

Location

Agency.com London, 85 Strand, London WC2R 0DW.
Additional offices in Amsterdam, New York, Chicago,
Dallas, and San Francisco.

Contact

info.London@agency.com

Awards

Revolution 2004 Best Consumer Marketing, CIM Travel Advertising
Awards 2004 (Gold/Silver) and IAB Creative Showcase winners.

Clients

3M, British Airways, British Telecom, Cahoot, Dulux, eBay,
HP, Heineken, Miller Brewing Company, NSPCC, Sainsbury's
Bank, T-Mobile, VISA, etc.

ARTLESS

\<JAPAN\>

www.artless.gr.jp

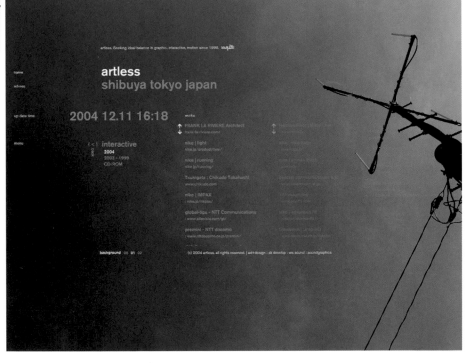

Concept

Artless, seeking ideal balance in graphic, interactive, motion... //// Naturellement, rechercher l'équilibre idéal entre graphisme, interactivité et animation... //// Ohne Schnörkel, auf der Suche nach der idealen Balance in Grafik, Interaktivität, Bewegung...

www.artless.gr.jp

Name artless Inc.

Founded 2002

Team 1 Art Director/Graphic Designer/Photographer, 1 Graphic/Web Designer, 1 Painter, and many freelance members and partner-companies/units (Flash Designer, Programmer, Photographer, Illustrator, VJ, DJ, Sound Designer, Motion Designer, Products Designer, Planer, Artist...).

Tools Html and Macromedia Flash.

Location

55 Park Axis 1-4-7 Shibuya
Shibuya-ku, 150-0002 Tokyo
Japan

Contact

info@artless.gr.jp

Awards

The Web Design Award 1999 (nomination), The Web Design Award
2002 (nominated), Web Design Index Award (grand prize), Good
Design Award (nomination), and more...

Clients

Nike Japan, +81 magazine, Dentsu, Fronteg Inc, Sony, JVC,
Macromedia, amana, Docomo, Steelcase Inc, IDEE, NTT,
MTV, NHK, etc.

ASTERIK STUDIO

‹USA›

www.asterikstudio.com

Concept

Style vs. Functionality (the process of uniting beauty and business). //// Style vs. fonctionnalité (la conjugaison de la beauté et du commerce). //// Stil versus Funktionalität (Der Prozess, Schönheit und Geschäft zu vereinen).

www.banduilder.com/shrek2

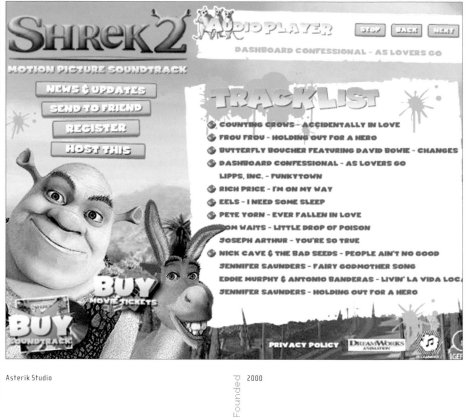

Name Asterik Studio

Founded 2000

Team 2 Art Directors, 1 Programmer, and 3 Designers.

Tools Macromedia Dreamweaver, Macromedia Fireworks, Macromedia Flash, Adobe Illustrator, and Adobe Photoshop.

Location 3524 West Government Way
Seattle WA 98199
USA

Contact info@asterikstudio.com

Awards Asterik Studio has received recognition from numerous
publications, tutorials and award competitions.

Clients Interscope Records, Geffen Records, Elektra Records, EMI Records,
Dreamworks Records, Atlantic Records, Universal Records, Eminem,
Black Eyed Peas, Sugababes, All-American Rejects, Pedro the Lion,
The Strokes, The White Stripes, Jimmy Eat World, Jessica Simpson,
Kid Rock, The Used, Brand New, Bright Eyes, Van Halen, etc.

ATMOSPHERE CPH

‹DENMARK›

www.atmosphere-cph.com

From Atmosphere with love! //// Bons baisers d'Atmosphere! //// Atmosphäre mit Liebe kreiert!

www.theword.dk

Name Atmosphere Cph

Founded 2000

Team 2 Strategic Planners, 3 Account Managers, 5 Creative/Designers, 3 Technical Developers ...and a robot monkey.

Tools Macromedia Flash, Discreet 3D Studio Max, Apple Final Cut Pro, html, C#, and VB.NET.

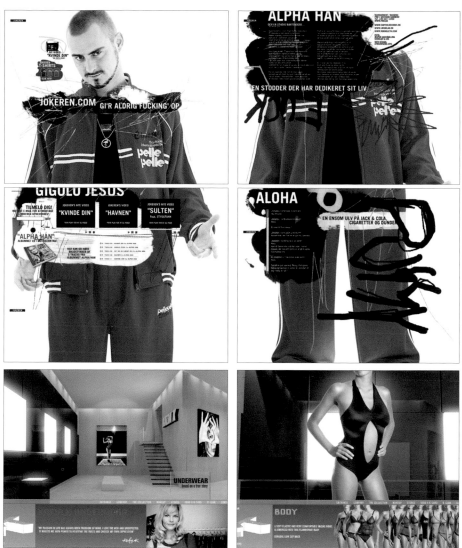

Store Kongensgade 72, 1 st floor
1264 Copenhagen
Denmark

info@atmosphere-cph.com

Cannes Cyber Lion, The One Show (Gold), The New York Festival:
Gold/Silver (various), Danish Creative Circle Award (various), etc.

Amnesty International, Braun, Danish Gambling Association,
Gillette, Helena Rubinstein, House of Prince, Jokeren, Jägermeister,
Maersk (Broker, Sealand, Logistics), Masterfoods (Whiskas, Uncle
Bens, Sheba, Snickers, M&M's), Oracle Denmark, Skandia Pension,
Smirnoff Ice, Telco Sensors, The Army, The Word, Yellow Pages, etc.

AVENUE A/RAZORFISH

\<USA\>
www.avenuea-razorfish.com

Concept

Our work must not only be aesthetically compelling, it must also drive increased business and brand awareness for our clients. To meet this goal, our creative work is anchored in a strategic model that we call the Customer Experience Journey (CEJ). The CEJ is a framework for capturing and identifying online and offline levers that collectively move customers from the initial awareness of a brand through to brand loyalty and advocacy. //// Notre travail doit être plus qu'esthétiquement convaincant, il doit également accroître les affaires de nos clients ainsi que la notoriété de leur marque. En ce sens, notre travail créatif se base sur un modèle stratégique que nous appelons l'Aventure client (CEJ - Customer Experience Journey). La CEJ est un cadre de capture et d'identification des leviers en ligne et hors ligne qui transforment la notoriété initiale d'une marque en fidélité et défense de la marque par les clients. //// Unsere Arbeit muss nicht nur auf ästhetischer Ebene herausragend sein, sie muss ausserdem extremen Geschäftssinn und Produktbewusstsein für unsere Kunden bieten. Um dieses Ziel zu erreichen, ist unsere kreative Arbeit in einem strategischen Modell verankert, das wir die Kundenerfahrungsreise (CEJ - Customer Experience Journey) nennen. Diese Erfahrungsreise ist ein Netzwerk, um Markenträger on- und offline zu erfassen und zu identifizieren. Nach einem anfänglichen Markenbewusstsein werden unsere Kunden zu treuen Befürwortern des Produktes.

www.postopia.com

Name Avenue A | Razorfish

Founded 1997 *Both Avenue A and Razorfish were founded in 1997, but only recently -July 2004- merged together.

Team Large number of professionals in all creative and management areas.

Tools Macromedia Dreamwever, Macromedia Flash, Flex MX, Homesite, Adobe Photoshop, Adobe Illustrator, Adobe InDesign, Adobe goLive, Apple Final Cut Pro, Cinema 4D, Sound Forge, Adobe After Effects, Macromedia Director, and Macromedia Fireworks.

Location

821 Second Avenue, 18th Floor
Seattle, WA 98104 - USA (headquarters)

Avenue A/Razorfish though has offices in 11 cities across the U.S.

Contact

info@avenuea-razorfish.com

Awards

Web Marketing Association (various), Marketing and Advertising
Awards (Finalist), MediaPost Creative Media Awards (Finalist),
International Web Page Awards (various), BDA Design Awards 2004,
Medicine on the Net: Web Excellence Awards (various), eHealthcare
Leadership Awards, Advertising Age, etc.

Clients

AstraZeneca, Best Buy, Kraft, Microsoft/MSN, Wells Fargo, etc.

INTERONE WORLDWIDE
<GERMANY/INTERNATIONAL>
www.interone.de

Concept Probably the most innovative agency of the world. //// *Sans doute l'agence la plus innovante au monde.* //// Wahrscheinlich die erfinderischste Agentur der Welt.

www.eplus-unlimited.de

Name INTERONE WORLDWIDE

Founded 2000

Team 400 Employees around the world (180 creatives).

Tools No favourite tool.

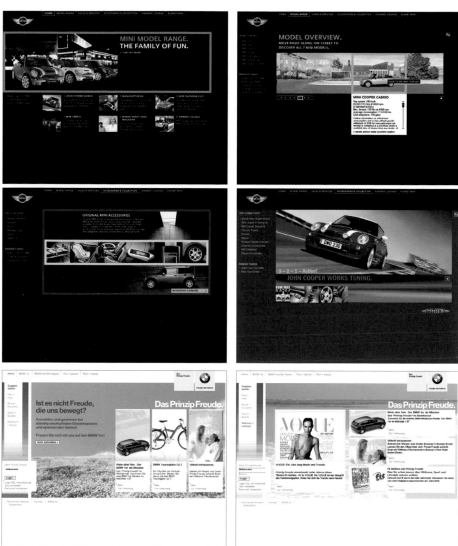

www.mini.com

www.prinzipfreude.de

Location

Headquarter: INTERONE WORLDWIDE, Sandstrasse 33, 80335
Munich; Germany

Offices in Cologne, Berlin, Hamburg, Düsseldorf, Bangkok and Peking.

Awards

Cannes Direct Lion (Gold), Cannes Cyber Lions: Silver (various),
Cresta Award, NY Festival Award, DDP Awards: Gold/Silver/Bronze
(various), etc.

Contact

martin.hubert@interone.de

thomas.knauer@interone.de

Clients

BMW, Mini, Deutsche Post World Net, LBS, Postbank,
Boehringer-Ingelheim, Allianz, E-Plus, RTL, etc.

BLITZ

Concept

BLITZ specializes in interactive experiences that elevate the medium, tapping into the emotions of consumers while exceeding the expectations of clients through flawless code, inventive formats, pioneering technologies, attention to detail and a focus on measurable success. //// BLITZ est spécialisé dans les expériences interactives qui anoblissent le média en s'immisçant dans les émotions des consommateurs, tout en dépassant leurs attentes par le biais d'un code irréprochable, de formats inventifs, de technologies pionnières, du souci du détail et d'un objectif de succès quantifiable. //// BLITZ ist spezialisiert in interaktiver Erfahrung und steigert das gesamte Niveau dieses Mediums, indem die Gefühle der Verbraucher angerührt werden und die Erwartungen der Kunden durch Perfektion, einfallsreiche Formate, technische Pionierarbeit, Detailtreue sowie einem Schwerpunkt auf messbarem Erfolg übertroffen werden.

www.livethesaga.com

Name BLITZ

Founded 2001

Team Large team compased by Artists, Designers, Engineers, Programmers, IAs, Project and Account Managers, Musical Talents, and Marketing Strategists.

Tools Adobe After Effects, Illusion, Discreet 3D Studio Max, Sorenson Squeeze, etc.

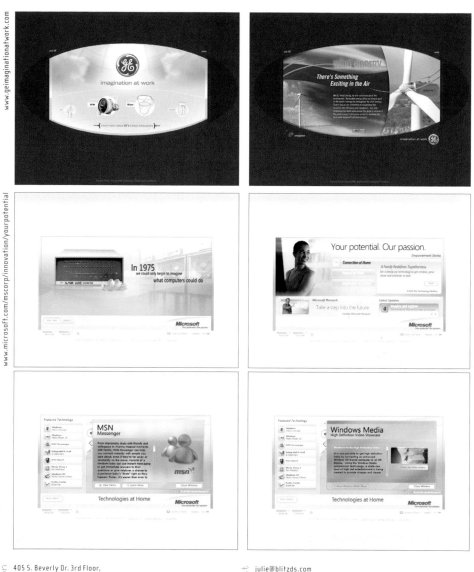

Location

405 S. Beverly Dr. 3rd Floor,
Beverly Hills, CA 90212
USA

Contact

julie@blitzds.com

Awards

Web Award Competition: Best Entertainment Website/Outstanding
Website, Internet Advertising Competition 2004 (Best
Entertainment Integrated Advertising Campaign), ADDYS 2004
(Silver Level), etc.

Clients

General Electric Company, LucasArts, Microsoft, Nintendo, Sony
Pictures Entertainment, Time Warner, Vivendi Universal Games, etc.

CRASHSHOP

<USA>

www.crashshop.com

Concept Air. Fuel. Compression. Spark. //// Air. Carburant. Compression. Etincelle. //// Luft. Treibstoff. Druck. Funken.

www.crashshop.com

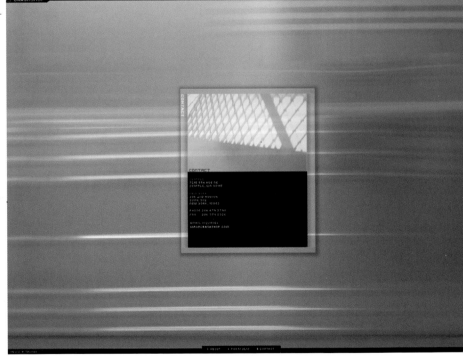

Name CrashShop

Founded 2001

Team 2 Art Directors, 2 Flash Designers, and 2 Programmers.

Tools Macromedia Flash, Adobe Photoshop, Adobe After Effects, Apple Final Cut Pro, Apple DVD Studio Pro, and Sorenson Squeeze.

Location 7215 5th Ave NE
Seattle, WA 98115
USA

Contact info@crashshop.com

Awards Print Magazine: Interaction Design Annual (Design Excellence Award), How Magazine Award, Interactive Competition Outstanding Award, Merit Award, and FS Award.

Clients Arch Projects, Agathos Foundation, Handsblue, J. Mendel (Paris), Krei Architecture, Neverstop, Mikco+, Yelena Yemchuk, Sci-Fi Channel, Cyclone Design, Sub Pop Records, Nabe Press

CUBAN COUNCIL

<USA>

www.cubancouncil.com

cuban council

Concept We specialize in creating simply superb solutions for web & print & such. //// Nous sommes spécialisés dans la création de solutions tout simplement grandioses pour Web & Print et autres. //// Wir sind darauf spezialisiert, einfach geniale Lösungen für Web & Printmedien & ähnliche Dinge zu erstellen.

www.k10k.net

Name Cuban Council

Founded 2002

Team 2 Designers/Art Directors, and 2 Programmers.

Tools Html, xhtml, CSS, JS, php, and Asp.Net.

Location

1201 Howard Street, Suite B
San Francisco, CA 94117
USA

Contact

fidel@cubancouncil.com

Awards

Mentions & interviews in more than 40 books & magazines, various
design awards over the years.

Clients

Apple, Adobe, Epitaph Records, Bell, Native Instruments,
Dadaphonic, etc.

D.WORKZ

\<USA\>

www.dworkz.com

Practical usability in original design style. //// La convivialité associée à un design original. //// Praktische Anwendung in originalem Design.

www.dworkz.com

Name — D.Workz Interactive

Founded — 2004

Team — 1 Art Director/Flash Designer, 1 Technical Director/Developer, 1 Developer, and 5 Contractors.

Tools — Macromedia Flash, Adobe Photoshop, Discreet 3D Studio Max, Action Script 2.0, amfphp, MySQL, Apache, XML, Javascript, Macromedia Director, Lingo, etc.

www.winelearningcenter.com

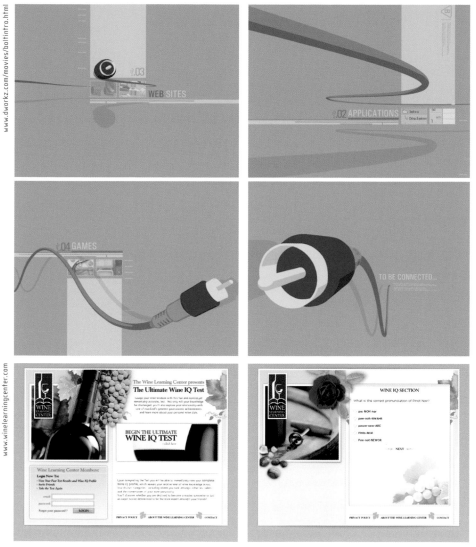

Location

360 Fillmore st.
San Francisco, CA 94117
USA

Contact

info@dworkz.com

Awards

Internet TINY Award (featured site), Minethink.com (cool site),
DopeAwards.com (professional), BestFlashDesigns.com (site of
the day), BlueIdea.com, fcukstar.com AWARD (site of the day),
and FWA (site of the day)

Clients

Sony, Yahoo!, CocaCola, mcDonalds, Marriott, Veritas, Cisco,
eAladdin,Sanrad, etc.

TRIBAL DDB
‹USA/INTERNATIONAL›
www.tribalddb.com

Concept

Simply put, we plan, build and sell our clients' brands online by generating Brand Demand. This means we begin by understanding our clients' businesses and the mindset of their customers. Then we provide concepts and strategies aimed at connecting the two and increasing desire: Generating Brand Demand. Finally, we creatively execute our concepts and provide full accountability of demand generated for dollars spent. //// En un mot comme en cent, nous concevons, créons et vendons en ligne les marques de nos clients en générant une demande pour ces dernières. Autrement dit, nous commençons d'abord par comprendre l'activité de nos clients et la façon de fonctionner de leurs clients. Nous proposons ensuite des concepts et des stratégies visant à relier les deux et à augmenter l'envie : c'est ce que nous appelons "générer une demande pour la marque". Pour finir, nous mettons en application nos concepts avec créativité et assumons la pleine responsabilité de la demande générée par l'argent investi. //// Ganz einfach, wir planen, erstellen und verkaufen die Produkte unserer Klienten, indem wir eine Produktnachfrage schaffen. Das bedeutet, zuerst setzen wir uns mit dem Geschäft unserer Klienten und der Denkweise ihres Kundenstammes auseinander. Dann stellen wir Konzepte sowie Strategien bereit, die darauf abgestimmt sind, diese beiden Faktoren zu verbinden, sowie das Bedürfnis zu verstärken: Wir schaffen Produktnachfrage. Zum Schluss führen wir auf kreativem Weg unsere Konzepte aus und übernehmen bei Nachfrage volle Verantwortung für jeden investierten Dollar.

www.volkswagen.com.au/site/R32/default.asp

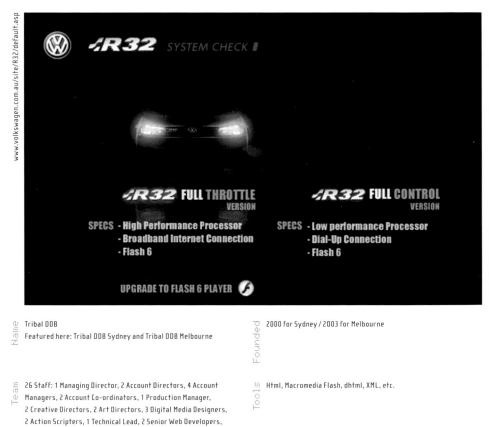

Name

Tribal DDB
Featured here: Tribal DDB Sydney and Tribal DDB Melbourne

Founded

2000 for Sydney / 2003 for Melbourne

Team

26 Staff: 1 Managing Director, 2 Account Directors, 4 Account Managers, 2 Account Co-ordinators, 1 Production Manager, 2 Creative Directors, 2 Art Directors, 3 Digital Media Designers, 2 Action Scripters, 1 Technical Lead, 2 Senior Web Developers, 2 Programmers, 1 Finance Manager, and 1 Accountant.

Tools

Html, Macromedia Flash, dhtml, XML, etc.

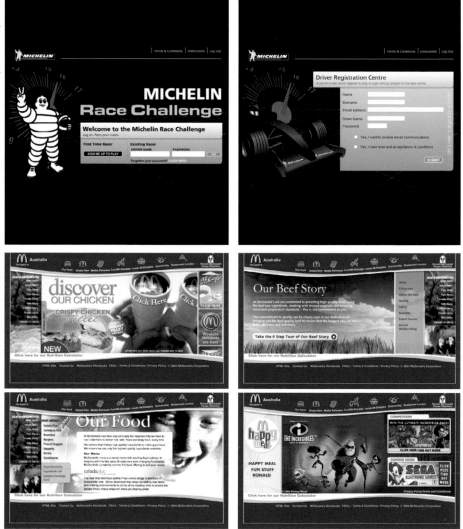

Worldwide network of 21 offices around the world.
Please refer to website. Featured sites are from the
Sidney office (www.tribalddb.com.au)

Contact info@tribalddb.com.au

Awards Golden Award of Montreux, MMA Awards, Web Award (various), Melb
Advert & Design Club (various), New York Festival (various), etc.

Clients Gatorade, McDonald's, Heinz Watties, Wrigley, Konica Minolta,
Kmart, Australian Unity, Volkswagen, Michelin, Alliance Property
Finance, CCS Index, HOBAN Recuitment, FlyBuys, ANZ, Jumbuck,
Mobil, Philips Medical, Schering Plough, Johnson & Johnson,
Schwarzkopf, Origins, Hocking Stuart, AVJennings, etc.

▦DENTSU

<JAPAN>

www.dentsu.com

Concept

Interactivity is fun, as is the joy of creating! But for the very same reasons, interactivity represents something more daunting for us. Viewers may be able to sit passively watching TV commercials films, but with most websites that's just not possible. Everyday we strive to create new ideas so as not to have people say, "How do you expect me to click on something when there is nothing creative there". //// L'interactivité c'est fun, tout comme l'est le plaisir de créer ! Mais l'interactivité est le défi qui nous motive le plus. Si un téléspectateur peut regarder passivement des films publicitaires, une telle passivité n'est pas compatible avec la plupart des sites Internet. Jour après jour, nous nous efforçons à créer de nouvelles idées afin que personne ne puisse dire : "Comment pouvez-vous attendre de moi que je clique sur quelque chose, il n'y a rien de créatif ici". //// Interaktivität macht Spass, sowie die Freude am Kreieren! Aber genau deshalb sehen wir Interaktivität als Herausforderung an. Zuschauer können ganz einfach passiv vor dem Fernseher sitzen und Werbefilme sehen, aber mit den meisten Webseiten geht das nicht. Täglich bemühen wir uns, neue Ideen zu kreieren, so dass keiner sagen kann "Wie kannst Du von mir erwarten, etwas anzuklicken, wenn es überhaupt nichts Kreatives anzuklicken gibt".

www.do-not-zzz.com

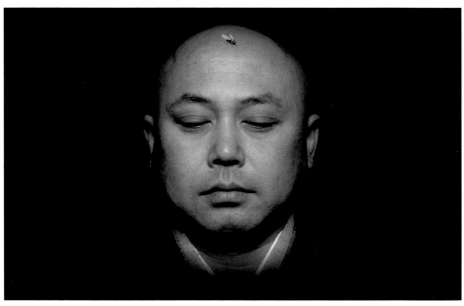

Name

DENTSU INC.

Founded

1901 (Dentsu's Interactive Creative Department was established in 1997.)

Team

3 Creative Directors, 2 Art Directors, 3 Web Planners, 2 Copy Writers, and 2 Flash Designers.

Tools

Macromedia Flash, XML, etc. Of course, that's what we do. But we believe that humor is more effective than any digital tools.

Is true beauty complicated?

wabi   dentsu   sabi

Is true beauty imperfect?

wabi   dentsu   sabi

Location

1-8-1, Higashi-shimbashi
Minato-ku, 105-7001 Tokyo
Japan

Awards

Cannes (Silver), The One Show (Gold), New Media Invision
Awards (Gold), etc.

Contact

Please refer to website.

Clients

Undisclosed.

DIGIT

<UK>

www.digitlondon.com

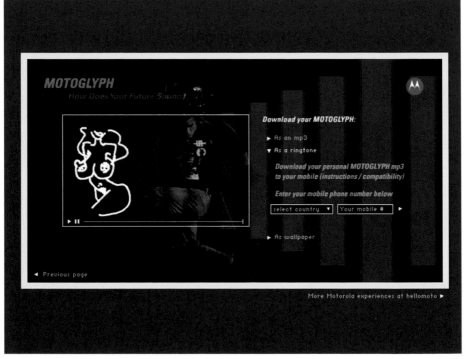

Concept

Digit uses real world tactility to express communication in the digital world. Simple. Human. Interaction. //// Digit utilise la tangibilité du monde réel pour exprimer la communication dans le monde numérique. Simplicité. Humanité. Interaction. //// Digit gebraucht wahren Spürsinn, um in der digitalen Welt zu kommunizieren. Einfach. Menschlich. Interaktiv.

www.digitlondon.com/motoglyph

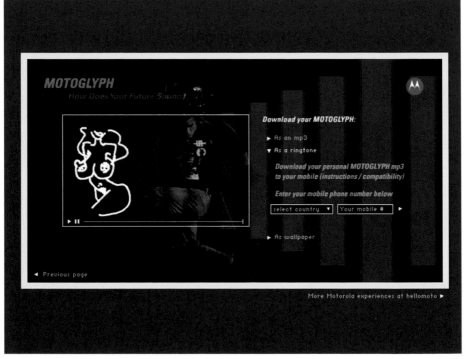

Name Digit

Founded 1996

Team 1 Art Director, 1 MD, 1 Commercial Director, 2 Art Directors, 2 Senior Designers, 7 Designers, 2 Production, 5 Technical Development, 2 Interaction Designers, 4 Account Producers, 1 Communications, and 2 Administrators/Office Management.

Tools Macromedia Flash, Macromedia Director, Discreet 3D Studio Max, and more...

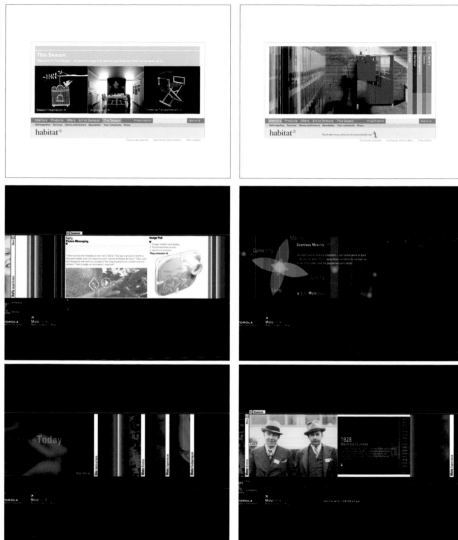

Location Jack's Place, Corbet Place
London E1
United Kingdom

Contact info@digitlondon.com

Awards Cannes Cyber Lions (Bronze), Winner BIMA, Design Week (various),
Annual Art Directors Club (various), D&AD: Silver (various),
Clio Awards (various), BIMA, Interactive BAFTA (various),
IVCA/Biz (net Award), London Interactive Advertising Award,
FlashForward, BDA (various), etc.

Clients Stella McCartney, The Place, Habitat, Mosaic Housing, Fabris Lane,
Bullrun, St.Lukes, Sky+, Moving Picture Company, Rizer, Hopkins,
Dido (BMG), Will Young, Motorola, Vodafone, The Public, Sorrell
Foundation, Red Cell, Erasmus Partners, Cinnamon Club, Warwick
Arts, NHSU, The Media Centre, etc.

DOMANI STUDIOS

<USA>

www.domanistudios.com

Concept

When designing for the web we push ourselves to find a balance between "look" and "touch". We take the most pride in those projects that allow us to blend communication design, motion graphics, and usability in a space where the elements harmonize with each other in new ways. //// Lorsque nous concevons des pages Web, nous nous efforçons de trouver l'équilibre entre le visuel et la fonctionnalité. Nous tirons la plus grande fierté des projets dans lesquels nous avons réussi à mixer communication, design, graphismes animés et convivialité dans un espace où les éléments s'harmonisent les uns avec les autres de façon novatrice. //// Wenn wir für das Web designen, versuchen wir, eine Balance zwischen "look" und "touch" herzustellen. Besonders wichtig sind uns solche Projekte, die es uns erlauben, Kommunikationsdesign, Bewegungsgraphiken sowie Anwendungsmöglichkeiten dort zu kombinieren, wo Elemente auf neue Weise miteinander harmonieren.

whotels

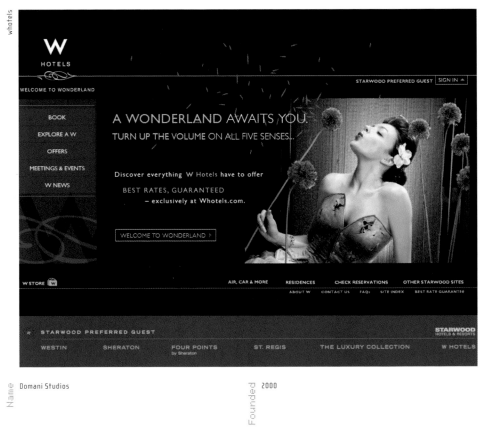

Name Domani Studios

Founded 2000

Team 16 Employees, ranging from Strategy and Creative Directors to Database Programmers and Flash gurus.

Tools Macromedia Flash, ActionScript 2, XML, php, Java, MySQL, Linux, Adobe After Effects, etc.

Location

55 Washington St. Suite 822
Brooklyn, New York, NY 11201
USA

Contact

jon@domanistudios.com

Awards

ID Magazine Interactive Design Review (Gold), Summit Creative
Awards (Silver/Bronze), HOW Magazine Interactive Deign
Competition (Silver), Communication Arts/Design Interact 50W
(various), FWA (various), etc.

Clients

American Federation for the Arts, Clicquot Inc., CNBC, Esteé
Lauder/Bumble & Bumble, Geffen Records, Gucci, Lavett & Chin
Apothecaries, Philippe Adec, Starwood Hotels and Resorts, UBS/
Paine Webber, W Hotels, Weizmann Institute of Science,
Westin Hotels, Whitney Museum of Art, etc.

DOUBLEYOU

<SPAIN>

www.doubleyou.com

Concept

We establish a new relation between the brands and their targets in which every communication turns into an experience. //// Nous établissons une nouvelle relation entre les marques et leurs cibles. Une relation dans laquelle chaque communication devient une aventure. //// Wir erstellen Beziehungen zwischen Produkten und ihren Zielgruppen, wobei jegliche Kommunikation zu einer besonderen Erfahrung wird.

www.doubleyou.com/festivals/audia3/index_eng.html

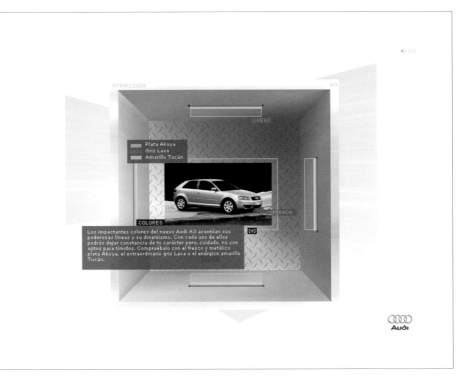

Name DoubleYou

Founded 1997

Team 2 Executive Creative Directors, 4 Creative Concept and Text, 2 Art Directors, 5 Designers, 2 Multimedia, 1 Interactive Creative Director, 3 Interactive Directors, 5 Programmers (Frontend), 1 Technical Director, 4 Programmers (Serverside), 2 Account Directors, and 4 Producers.

Tools Macromedia Flash, XML, dhtml, Adobe Ilustrator, Adobe Photoshop, Sorenson Squeeze, Microsoft Visual J++, ANT, Cygwin, etc.

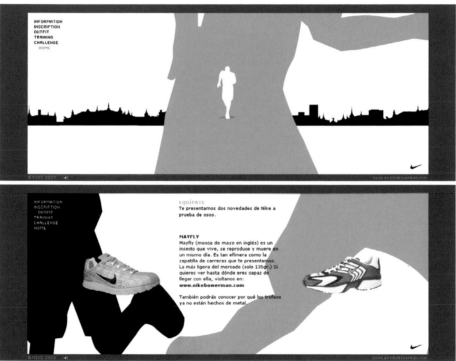

Location

Calle Església 4-10, 3-A
08024 Barcelona
Gran Vía 6, 6º, 28013 Madrid
Spain

Contact

barcelona@doubleyou.com
madrid@doubleyou.com

Awards

Cannes: Grand Prix/Cyber Lions (various), One Show Interactive: Gold/Silver (various), FIAP: Gold/Bronze (various), Clio Awards (Bronze), London Festival: Gold/Finalist (various), IAAA: Gold/Silver/Bronze (various), El Sol Festival (San Sebastián), etc.

Clients

Arbora & Ausonia, Audi, Bimbo, Danone, Diesel, Dodot, Eastpack, Electronic Arts, Esteve, Evax, Fontwella, Lanjaron, Myrurgia, Nestle, Nike, San Miguel, Seat, Yahoo!, Iberia, etc.

DRAFT DIGITAL

<USA>
www.draftdigital.com

Concept Draft Digital fuses brand strategy, cutting-edge technology, and a rich legacy of direct marketing experience to create results-driven interactive solutions. //// Draft Digital fait fusionner stratégie de marque, technologie d'avant-garde et grande expérience du marketing direct pour créer des solutions interactives tournées vers le résultat. //// Draft Digital verbindet Produktstrategien, einschneidende Technologien sowie ein reiche Erfahrung im Direktmarketing, um gezielte interaktive Lösungen zu erreichen.

www.snuggle.com

Name Draft Digital

Founded 1999

Team 1 Creative Director, 1 Associate Creative Director, 2 Senior Designer, 2 Flash Developer, 3 Copywriter, 1 Developer, 1 Production Designer, 2 Account Director, and 5 Producer.

Tools Adobe Photoshop, Macromedia Flash, Adobe After Effects, XML, pencil and paper.

Location

919 Third Avenue
New York, NY 10022
USA

Contact

kaktulun@draftnet.com

Awards

Standard of Excellence Award (various), Outstanding Website Award
draftworldwide.com Standard of Excellence Award, Best Consumer
Goods Website, Echo Trophy (Winner), etc

Clients

Aarp/Unitedhealth Group, Audi of America, Avis, Bank of America,
Hewlett-Packard, Johnson & Johnson, Jose Cuervo, Target, Verizon
Wireless, etc.

DRAWING AND MANUAL
<JAPAN>
www.drawingandmanual.com

Concept.

The design which pulls out the feature of a company. The design which adds new value by web. The design based on new inventiveness. ////
Un design qui met en vedette l'image de marque des entreprises. Un design qui donne de la valeur ajoutée par le biais du Net. Un design basé sur une nouvelle inventivité. //// Design, das die Charakteristiken einer Firma hervorhebt. Design, das neue Werte zum Web hinzufügt. Design, basierend auf neuen Erfindungen.

www.karimoku60.com

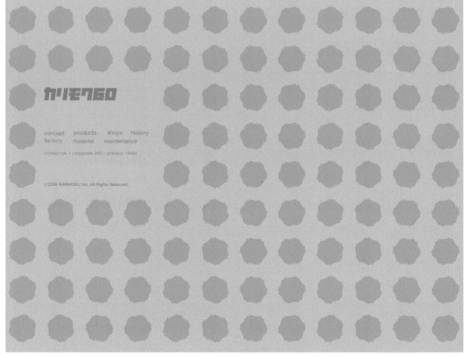

Name	DRAWING AND MANUAL	Founded	1997
Team	1 Producer, 1 Director, 3 Designers, and 1 Programmer.	Tools	Anything.

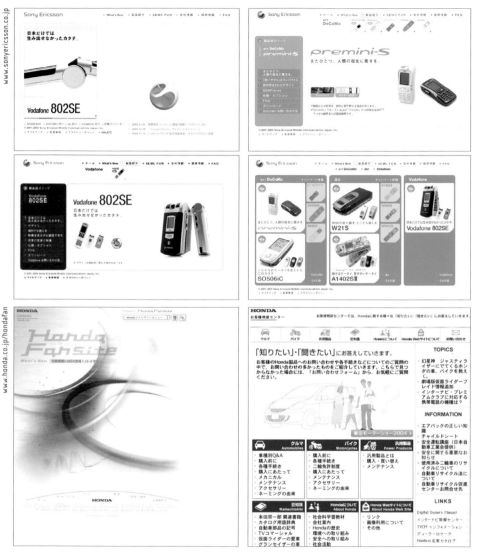

www.honda.co.jp/hondafan

New York ADC Merit, International Broadcasting Awards
(Finalist), etc.

Location
Okusawa 8-3-2
Setagaya-ku, 158-0083 Tokyo
Japan

Contact
info@drawingandmanual.com

Clients
Honda, Sony, Sony Ericsson Mobile Communications, etc.

EMILIANO RODRÍGUEZ

<ARGENTINA>

www.emilianorodriguez.com.ar

Concept

I try to keep things simple. If you have a strong concept then you don't need to fill the screen with unnecessary graphics that will surely confuse the visitor. I think that powerful ideas have simple resolutions. "Less is more". //// J'essaie de faire simple. Si votre concept est fort, inutile de remplir l'écran de graphismes superflus qui ne feront certainement que troubler le visiteur. Pour moi, aux bonnes idées doit correspondre une mise en pratique simple. "Il faut jouer la carte de l'économie". //// Ich versuche, die Dinge einfach zu halten. Wenn du ein solides Konzept hast, dann brauchst du den Bildschirm nicht mit überflüssigen Grafiken zu füllen, die sowieso nur den Besucher verwirren. Ich denke, gute und starke Ideen lassen sich einfach umsetzen. "Weniger ist mehr".

Name Emiliano Rodríguez Ruiz de Gauna

Founded 2002

Team I'm a one-man studio but am constantly incorporating different professionals to the projects according to the needs.

Tools Html, dhtml, XML, and Macromedia Flash.

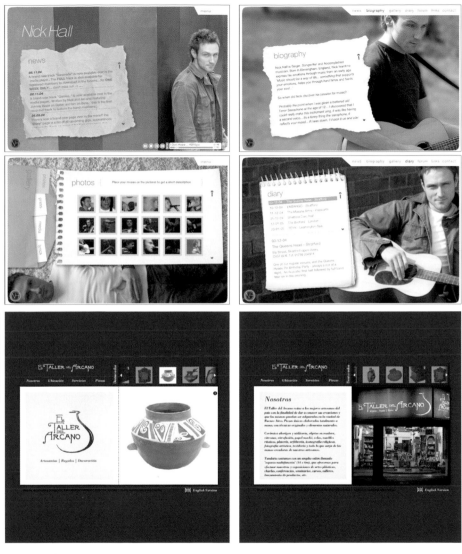

www.nick-hall.com

www.tallerdelarcano.com.ar

Location

Manzanares 1831 1°C

1429 Buenos Aires

Argentina.

Contact

emi@emilianorodriguez.com.ar

Awards

Netdiver.net, American Design Awards, fcukstar.com, DOPE Awards, 2 stars in plasticpilots.com, Design Taxi (Site of the Day), Newwebpick.com, 4efx, Site of the Week in e-creative.net, Webmaster Award in ab19.it.

Clients

Sony Latinamerica, JVC Futurevision (UK), Nick Hall (UK), Manchester City (UK), Monterey Mushrooms (USA), Media8 (USA), Elite Home Theater Seating (Canada), Funky Productions (Argentina), El Taller del Arcano (Argentina), etc.

EMPORIOASIA

<CHINA>

www.emporioasia.com

Concept EmporioAsia is one of China's leading interactive marketing agencies. We offer cutting-edge, high-quality work to mainly blue chip clients. //// EmporioAsia est l'une des plus grandes agences chinoises de marketing interactif. Nous proposons nos solutions haute qualité d'avant-garde principalement à des clients de premier ordre. //// EmporioAsia ist eine der führenden interaktiven Marketingagenturen Chinas. Wir bieten einschneidende, hochqualifizierte Arbeit für unsere vorwiegend 'blu chip'-Klientel.

www.bundcenter.com

Name EmporioAsia Inc.

Founded 1999

Team 10 to 20 Designers, Developers and Creative professionals in different areas.

Tools Macromedia Flash.

REGAL SHANGHAI EAST ASIA HOTEL
上海富豪東亞酒店

中文

HOME
RESERVATIONS
MAPS
ACCOMMODATION
FREQUENT FLYER PROGRAMS
LOYALTY PROGRAMS
DINING & ENTERTAINMENT
BANQUETING & CONVENTION
RECREATION
CAREERS
CONTACT US
SHANGHAI LINKS
REGAL HOTELS INTERNATIONAL

REGAL HAPPENINGS

GUEST ROOM OFFERS

Within the Shanghai Stadium in bustling Xu Hui District - where business and pleasure convene

The Regal Shanghai East Asia Hotel, an integrated part of the 80,000-seat multi functional Shanghai Sports Centre, is adjacent to the elevated inner ring road and next to the Stadium subway "Metro" station and Cao Xi Road Light Railway Station. An ideal location with convenient and fast access to all parts of Shanghai, airports and the suburban areas.

SHANGHAI WEATHER

SIGN-UP TO RECEIVE OUR LATEST SPECIAL OFFERS AND PROMOTIONS

Email:

SUBMIT

Powered by EmporioAsia

中文

Thai Smooth as silk

• Home
• News
• Flight Schedules
• About THAI
• Our Fleet
• THAI's Destinations
• Fly With Us
• Royal Orchid Holidays
• Royal Orchid Plus
• THAI Service
• Partners
• Contact Us

77 Destinations
34 Countries

Hot Deals for Shanghai

Powered by EmporioAsia

Location

Unit 5C, Jin Ming Building
8 Zun Yi Road South
200335 Shanghai
China

Contact

ask@emporioasia.com

Awards

None

Clients

Marriott, Hyatt, Hilton, Thai Airways, InterContinental, Starwood, TUI, GTA, etc.

ENGAGE

<UK>

www.engagestudio.com

Concept. An Idea, An Approach. //// Une idée, une approche. //// Eine Idee, Eine Annäherung.

www.universaldesignstudio.com

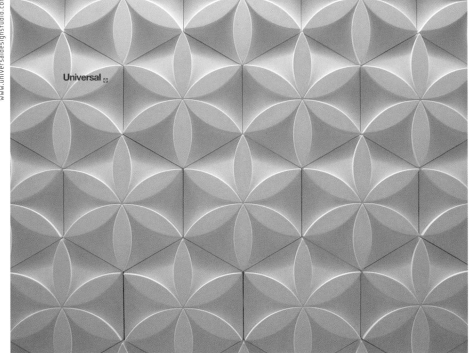

Name Engage

Founded 2001

Team A number of professionals in all creative and managament areas.

Tools Macromedia Flash, XML, php, etc.

56 · BEST STUDIOS

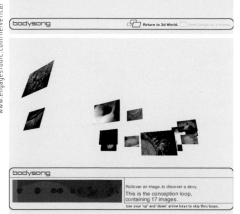

Anja's pregnant tummy
Source: Home Movies

1996 - Anja was seven months pregnant when this record of her pregnancy was filmed by her husband Patrick.

They are both photographers. He had recently bought a video camera and was trying it out.

Anja grew up beside a lake in Germany, and swam every week throughout her pregnancy. The feeling of the water taking the weight of her body from her was liberating, so she decided to have a water birth.

She hired a birthing pool and organised a home birth with an experienced midwife.

At the age of two her daughter fell into the lake while on holiday and almost drowned. In spite of this she is now a keen swimmer.

Link to related story:
Anja's pregnant pectie.

Helvetica vs. Arial

Helvetica was developed by the Haas Foundry of Switzerland in the 1950s. Microsoft distributed a typeface called Arial, a very similar typeface, that comes bundled with every desktop computer.

Thus Arial has now overtaken Helvetica as the standard font in practically everything done by those who don't know better.

Take the role of Helvetica, and let Arial know we don't need its type around here.

DIRECTIONS
Move your Helvetica character left and right with the mouse, beat Arial by jumping on it using the mouse button. Helvetica moves faster in flight.

HELVETICA;
HOMAGE TO A TYPEFACE
Lars Müller Publishers
Hardcover - November 2002
BUY ONLINE

TOGGLE QUALITY HI MED LO

Helvetica

Helvetica
abcdefhiklmnorstuvwxz
987654321

Arial
abcdefhiklmnorstuvwxz
987654321

engage

bodysong Rollover an image, to discover a story.
This is the conception loop, containing 17 images.
Use your 'up' and 'down' arrow keys to skip thru loops.

Location
45 Carnaby Street
London W1F 9PR
United Kingdom

Contact
info@engagestudio.com

Awards
The British Academy of Film & Television Arts.

Clients
Sony Computer Entertainment, Toshiba Mobile Communications, Nokia, Orange, D&AD, The Mill, Hot Property Films, Universal Design Studio, Barber Osgerby, Mode, etc.

EVER GROWING

<USA/UK>

www.evergrowing.net

EGS

EGS

Concept: Always blossoming, developing and thriving. Ever Growing. //// En évolution et ébullition perpétuelles. Toujours plus haut. //// Immer blühend, sich weiterentwickelnd und erfolgreich. Ever growing - stets im Wachstum begriffen.

www.nikesoccer.com/tape

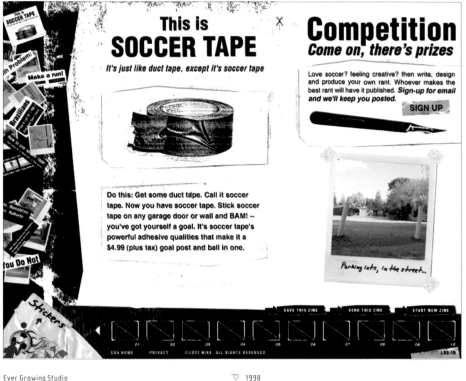

Name: Ever Growing Studio

Founded: 1998

Team: Creative Director, Communications Consultant and Publicist, Art Director, 3 Designers, 2 Interactive Designers, Programmer and Software Engineer.

Tools: Adobe Photoshop, Adobe Illustrator, Macromedia Flash, html, dhtml, CSS, etc.

www.silasandmaria.com

www.wskartists.com

Location

1729 Palm Avenue, San Mateo
CA, 94402 - USA
12 Healey Street
London NW1 8SR, United Kingdom

Awards

Communication Arts: Interactive Award for Advertising, Macromedia
[Site of the Day], FWA ONE Award, Flash GFX [Stunning Site],
Netdiver Network [Explorative Site], The ISI Award for Business To
Business Marketing Online at the BIMA Awards, etc.

Contact

arron@evergrowing.net

Clients

BBC, Microsoft, Universal Records, Nike, Virgin Music, Naked
Communications, EMI, Silas and Maria, Venables, Bell & Partners,
Ministry of Sound, etc.

EXOPOLIS

\<USA\>

www.exopolis.com

Concept

The exportation of creative concept to the world market. //// L'exportation de concepts créatifs sur le marché mondial. //// Export von kreativen Konzepten im Weltmarkt.

www.resfest.com

resfest | 2004
DIGITAL FILM FESTIVAL

» PRESS   » SPONSORS   » ABOUT RESFEST   » STORE   » PROGRAM GUIDE

TOUR DATES   TICKETS   FILMS   LIVE MUSIC   EVENTS   WEBLOG

new york city	los angeles	washington, d.c.	zurich	melbourne	las palmas
boston	glasgow	dublin	cape town	barcelona	sydney
san francisco	portland	são paulo	osaka	madrid	istanbul
london	bristol	nottingham	johannesburg	valladolid	
sheffield	toronto	seoul	chicago	vigo	
austin	singapore	tokyo	fukuoka	vitoria	

CURRENTLY IN:

> **ISTANBUL**

RES-TANBUL
Arriving in the vast, ancient city of Istanbul was a shock to the system. The cab ride from Ataturk Airport to our hotel in the thriving commercial district of Beyoglu revealed a city literally built upon layers of history, with...

RESFEST ON KOREAN TV
Catch RESFEST festival director Jonathan Wells on the global English-language Korean TV network Arirang TV talking about this year's festival. The 30 minute daily interview show HEART TO HEART will also feature clips of highlights

Global Presenting Sponsor:
Panasonic
ideas for life

Name Exopolis

Founded 2002

Team 1 VP of Interactive Technology, 1 Creative Director, 1 Executive Producer Web Division, 1 Director of Interactive Technology, and 2 Web Designers.

Tools Macromedia Flash, Adobe Illustrator, Adobe Photoshop, XML, Adobe After Effects, etc.

Location
2019 Riverside Drive
Los Angeles CA 90039
USA

Contact
kat@exopolis.com

Awards
FWA, Bombshock Awards, Macromedia Site of the Day, etc.

Clients
Universal Pictures, Warner Bros. Pictures, J Records, S-Curve
Records, Blue Cult Jeans, Disney, Kids WB, Res Fest, etc.

EXTERA
<SAN MARINO REPUBLIC>
www.extera.com

The work, the engagement, and creativity of the design: the elements of a passion without limits that pushes to think always about open virtual spaces to us and to boost new ideas, shapes, and innovation. //// Le travail, l'engagement et la créativité du design : les éléments d'une passion sans limites, qui pousse à penser toujours des espaces virtuels ouverts à de nouvelles idées, à de nouvelles formes et à l'innovation. //// Die Arbeit, die Hingabe und die Kreativität im Design: alles Bestandteile einer grenzenlosen Hingabe und Überzeugung, die uns ständig treibt, neue virtuelle Ebenen, Ideen, Formen und Erkenntnisse zu erlangen.

www.extera.com

Name Extera srl

Founded 2000

Team 14 Professionals doing web design, graphics, flash design, programming, and web marketing.

Tools Macromedia Dreamweaver, Macromedia Flash, Visual Studio, etc.

Location

Via Onesto Scavino, 4 – 47891
Repubblica di San Marino

Contact

simon@extera.com

Awards

ADCI Art Director Club Italiano, Italian Web Award
(www.premiowebitalia.it), King for a Week
(www.kingforaweek.com), etc.

Clients

Terranova, Teddy, Ciesse Piumini, Albini & fontanot, Arke,
Electronics, Eplanet, Isoitalia, Cota&Tequila productions, etc.

FAHRENHEIT

‹USA›

www.fahrenheit.com

Concept With backgrounds in art and architecture, the web provides us an opportunity to practice our many disciplines in one media. We combine structurally precise navigation and striking use of colour to create an environment that is highly accessible and full of emotion. //// Le Net nous offre l'opportunité de mettre en pratique nos nombreuses compétences (en art et architecture notamment) dans un unique média. Nous conjuguons une navigation structurellement précise et l'usage marquant de couleurs pour créer des environnements hautement accessibles et pleins d'émotions. //// Mit Hintergrund in Kunst und Architektur, bietet uns das Web die Möglichkeit, unsere vielfältigen Kenntnisse in nur einem Medium anzuwenden. Wir kombinieren eine präzise durchstrukturierte Navigation mit auffälligen Farben, um eine Umgebung zu kreieren, die besonders gut zugänglich und voller Gefühl ist.

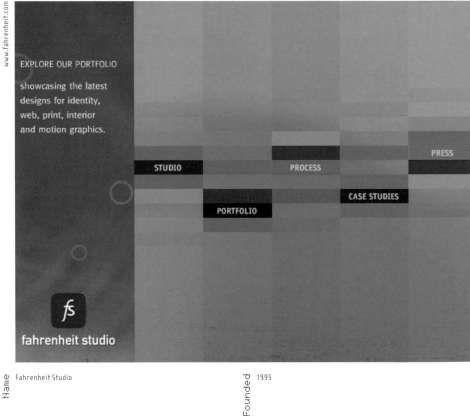

Name Fahrenheit Studio

Founded 1995

Team 2 Art Directors, 1 Flash Designer, and 1 Programmer.

Tools Html, Macromedia Flash, Javascript, etc.

Location

10303 Mississippi Avenue
Los Angeles, CA 90025
USA

Contact

info@fahrenheit.com

Awards

Creativity Award, Summit Award, Surfers Choice Award, Web
Marketing Association Award, World Best Web Sites Hall of Fame,
Macromedia Shock Site of the Day, Netscape France Flash Site of
the Day, etc.

Clients

IBM, Warner Bros, Warner Music Group, Sony Music, Mattel,
New Line, Fox Kids, etc.

FANTASY INTERACTIVE

\<SWEDEN\>

www.fantasy-interactive.com

Fantasy Interactive has a burning passion for interactive concepts, design and development. We provide leading companies worldwide with next generation Internet applications and designs, accommodating millions of users and allowing them to interact with the future, today. All Fantasy Interactive products are made to make a difference, and to make clients look anything but indifferent. //// Fantasy Interactive a une véritable passion pour les concepts, le design et le développement interactifs. Nous fournissons à des entreprises de premier plan du monde entier des applications et design Internet de nouvelle génération. Nous touchons ainsi des millions d'usagers et leur permettons de communiquer avec le futur, dès aujourd'hui. Tous les produits Fantasy Interactive sont créés pour faire la différence ainsi que pour susciter tout sauf l'indifférence chez les clients. //// Fantasy Interactive besitzt eine Leidenschaft für interaktive Konzepte, Design und Entwicklung. Wir liefern führenden Gesellschaften weltweit zukunftsorientierte Internet-Applikationen und Design, passend für Millionen von Nutzern, denen wir die Möglichkeit geben, bereits heute mit der Zukunft interaktiv zu werden. Alle Fantasy Interactive Produkte haben das gewisse Etwas und lassen den Kunden keinesfalls gleichgültig.

www.fordvehicles.com

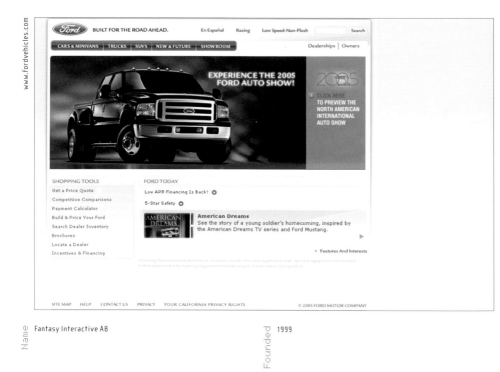

Name Fantasy Interactive AB

Founded 1999

Team 15 People, split into 4 divisions: Management: business, client management and project management; Art: 2D/3D, animation and video production; Interactive: interactive design and development; Tech: system architecture, system design and application development.

Tools Macromedia Flash, Adobe Photoshop, Adobe After Effects, Maya, and more...

Location

Brunnsgränd 4, P.O. Box 2265

103 17 Stockholm

Sweden

Contact

Camilla@fantasy-interactive.com

Awards

FWA Awards (various), Bombshock Awards/www.ultrashock.com (various), Macromedia Awards (various), Flash Forward Film Festival (various), etc.

Clients

Time Warner Cable/Road Runner, Microsoft, Ford Motor Company/J. Walter Thompson and Matthews International Corporation, etc.

FARFAR

farfar

Concept

We're Farfar and we create advertising on the Internet. Through the years we've concentrated on communicating to the audience's hearts and create linking, rather than branding. (A brief look at our collection of prizes could lead to the conclusion that we've been rather successful). But that shouldn't make you think that we don't understand the mechanics of a strong brand. On the contrary! We're not at all fans of funny things that serve no purpose. At least not when it comes to advertising. //// Nous sommes créateur de publicités pour l'Internet. Depuis des années, nous nous employons à nous adresser au cœur des internautes et à préférer les liens aux stratégies de marque. Il suffit de jeter un coup d'œil sur les récompenses que nous avons reçues pour se convaincre que cela nous a plutôt réussi. Mais ceci ne signifie pas que nous comprenons pas le fonctionnement des rouages d'une marque forte. Bien au contraire ! Nous ne sommes justes pas adeptes des fantaisies inutiles. Du moins en matière de publicité. //// Wir sind Farfar und machen Werbung im Internet. Über die Jahre hinweg haben wir uns eher darauf konzentriert, mit dem Herzen des Kunden zu kommunizieren und eine Verbindung herzustellen, als Markenzeichen zu setzen. (Ein kurzer Blick auf unsere Ansammlung von Preisen könnte als Hinweis auf unseren Erfolg dienen). Das heisst allerdings nicht, dass wir die Techniken zur Herstellung eines guten Produktes nicht beherrschen. Ganz im Gegenteil. Wir sind keinesfalls Befürworter von lustigem Schnickschnack, der keinerlei Nutzen hat. Zumindest nicht, wenn es um Werbung geht.

www.farfar.se/beststudios/ngage_snowtour

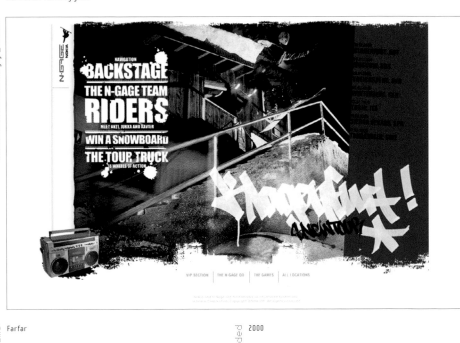

Name Farfar	**Founded** 2000	
Team A team of professionals in various creative and management areas.	**Tools** Macromedia Flash, Adobe Illustrator, Adobe Photoshop, Adobe After Effects, Discreet 3D Studio Max, Digital Camera, DV Camera, etc.	

Location

Bolinders Plan 2
112 24 Stockholm
Sweden

Contact

info@farfar.se

Awards

Cannes: Grand Prix/Gold/Bronze/Finalist (various), Clio Awards:
Silver/Shortlist (various), London Advertising Awards (Gold), Art
Directors Club NY (Silver), ID Magazine Interactive Review (Silver),
Golden Egg, etc.

Clients

Milko, Absolut Vodka, Nokia, Red Bull, Levi's, MTV Networks,
Swedish Red Cross, com hem (Sweden's largest TV, Broadband &
Phone supplier), SJ (The Swedish railroad company), Svenska Spel
(The biggest gambling firm in Sweden), etc.

FIRSTBORN

<USA>

www.firstbornmultimedia.com

Concept

We keep things simple. Hide elements, but leave them accessible. Subtract, allowing the most important elements to rise to the surface. The result is a clean, elegant and sophisticated user experience. //// Nous privilégions la simplicité. Nous masquons certains éléments tout en les maintenant accessibles. En soustrayant ces derniers aux regards, nous permettons aux éléments les plus importants d'être mis en valeur. Le résultat est une expérience utilisateur nette, élégante et sophistiquée. //// Wir halten die Dinge einfach. Verstecken Teile, die aber trotzdem leicht zugänglich bleiben. Wir minimalisieren und ermöglichen somit wichtigen Elementen an die Oberfläche zu treten. Das Ergebnis ist eine saubere, elegante und weitentwickelte Erfahrung für den Verbraucher.

www.firstbornmultimedia.com/websites/chr/crossfire.htm

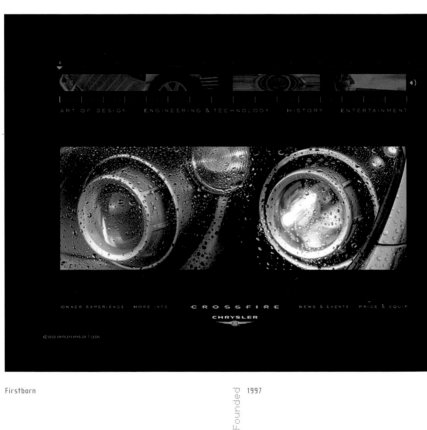

Name Firstborn

Founded 1997

Team 1 Creative Director, 2 Art Directors, 3 Flash Designers, 1 Production Artist, 1 Systems Analyst, 1 Director of Technology, 1 Senior Programmer, 3 Producers, and 2 Business Development Executives.

Tools Macromedia Flash, ActionScript, html, XML, asp, Asp.Net, Adobe Photoshop, Adobe Illustrator, Sound Forge, Charles, Adobe After Effects, Adobe Premiere, Sorenson Squeeze, php, MySQL, Discreet 3D Studio Max, V-ray, etc.

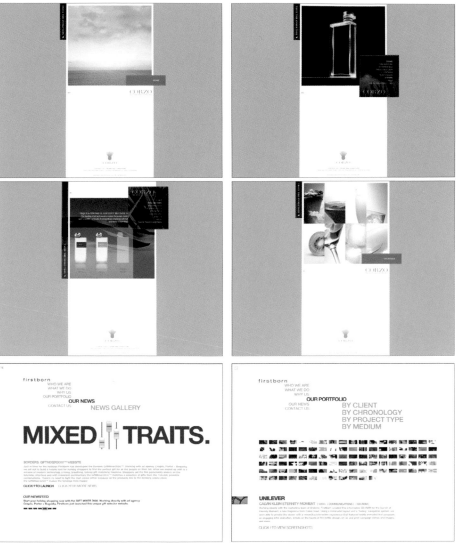

Location

630 9th Avenue, Suite 605
New York, NY 10036
USA

Contact

info@firstbornmultimedia.com

Awards

Communication Arts Interactive Annual: Winner (various),
HOW Magazine Interactive Design Competition: Winner (various),
Macromedia Site of the Day (various), Flashforward Flash Film
Festival (various), One Show Interactive Design Competition Merit
(Winner), Favorite Website Award: Winner (various), etc.

Clients

The Arnell Group, Atlantic Records, Bacardi USA, BBDO, Calvin
Klein, Clarins Fragrance Group, Columbia University, Estée Lauder,
Kerzner International, Kohn Pedersen Fox (KPF), L'Oréal, Madonna,
Museum of Modern Art, Ralph Lauren Fragrance, Sacha Biyan, Sci-Fi
Channel, Unilever, Victoria's Secret, Vitamin Water, Zirh, etc.

FISHOUSE

<**ITALY**>

www.fishouse.net

Concept

Fishouse is the brainchild of a team of professionals who want to redefine the rules of the game in online communication. The emotional impact of the Internet on the public is not usually built into any marketing strategy. We believe, however, that the Internet can be used effectively to arouse strong emotions, like any other medium. //// *Fishouse est la création d'une équipe de professionnels qui souhaitent redéfinir les règles du jeu de la communication en ligne. L'impact émotionnel d'Internet sur le public ne s'inscrit généralement dans aucune stratégie marketing. Nous croyons cependant qu'Internet peut être utilisé de manière efficace pour susciter de fortes émotions, comme tout autre média.* //// Fishouse ist das geistige Produkt eines professionellen Teams, das die Spielregeln der Online-Kommunikation redefinieren möchte. Der emotionale Einfluss des Internets auf die Öffentlichkeit ist normalerweise in keine Marketingstrategie mit eingebaut. Trotzdem sind wir davon überzeugt, dass das Internet effektiv dazu genutzt werden kann, – so wie viele andere Medien – starke Gefühle beim Publikum hervorzurufen.

www.thegarden.it

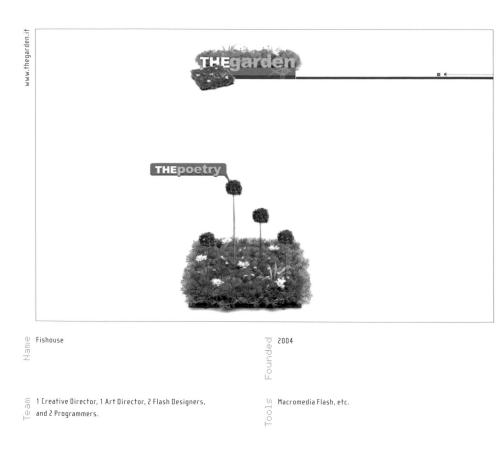

Name Fishouse

Founded 2004

Team 1 Creative Director, 1 Art Director, 2 Flash Designers, and 2 Programmers.

Tools Macromedia Flash, etc.

Awards **Location**

Via Romanina, 7 b 31033
Castelfranco Veneto (TV)
Italy

Mediastars (various), Interactive Key Award (www.mediakey.it) ,
Japan Media Arts Festival, Art Directors Club Italy, Flash Forward
Awards (various), etc.

Contact

info@fishouse.net

Clients

Warner Bros Italy, Sasch, Total Italy, Axo Sport, Clear Channel
Outdoor (Italy), Temavento, Zoogami, Flex, Alpieagles, Pianca,
Tubes. Fishouse, in addition developing its own projects,
collaborates with J. Walter Thompson Italy, Marketing Multimedia
Milan, Zanon & Partners and other advertising agencies.

FLUIDESIGN

<USA>

www.fluidesign.com

Concept Strikes an intelligent balance between technology and design across a gamut of industries. //// *Trouver le juste milieu entre technologie et design, toutes industries confondues.* //// Bietet einen intelligenten Ausgleich zwischen Technologie und Design in einer Vielzahl von Industriezweigen.

www.labellosangeles.com

Name Fluidesign

Founded 1998

Team 2 Designers, 2 html Programmers, 2 Programmers, 1 Sales Manager, 1 Copywriter, and 1 Leader.

Tools The usual Adobe/Macromedia/Apple products, Actionscript, php, CSS, XML, Canon 20d, Graph Paper, Thesaurus, etc.

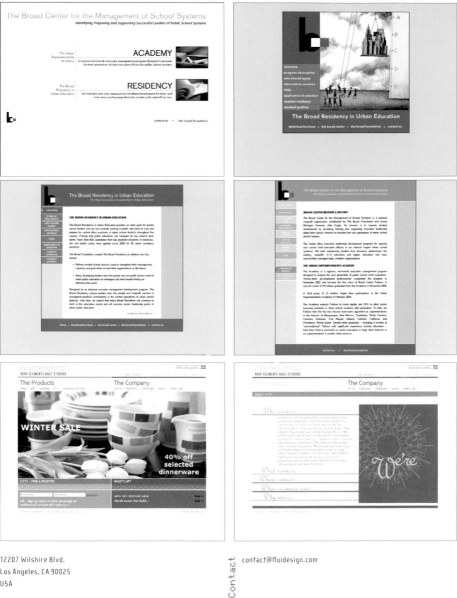

Location

12207 Wilshire Blvd.
Los Angeles, CA 90025
USA

Contact

contact@fluidesign.com

Awards

Small Business Administration's Young Entrepreneur of the Year.

Clients

The Broad Foundation, Technicolor, Fox Studios, RE/MAX
in California and Hawaii, Manatt, Phelps & Phillips,
General Motors, etc.

FORK

Concept

"Per aspera ad astra." (Through rough ways to the stars; through suffering to renown.) //// "Per aspera ad astra." (Par des sentiers ardus jusqu'aux étoiles.) //// "Per aspera ad astra." (Über steinige Wege die Sterne erreichen, nach langem Leiden endlich Anerkennung gewinnen.)

www.transmediale.de/04/page/home.0.1.html

Name Fork Unstable Media

Founded 1996

Team 1 Managing Partner, 1 Creative Partner, 1 Managing Director, 1 Creative Director, 1 Account Director, 1 Office Manager, 1 Office Assistant, 2 Frontdesk, 6 Account Manager, 2 Project Manager, 1 Content Manager, 1 Technical Project Manager, 1 System Administrator, 5 Programmer, 8 Designer, and 3 Copywriters.

Tools Xhtml, dhtml, CSS, XML, Macromedia Flash, php, MySQL, and alcohol.

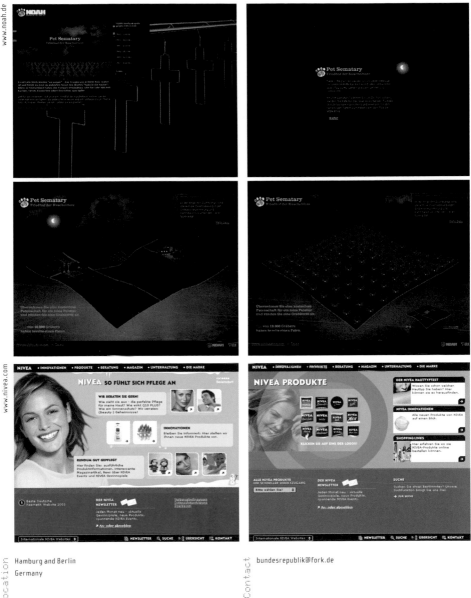

www.noah.de

www.nivea.com

Location

Hamburg and Berlin
Germany

Contact

bundesrepublik@fork.de

Awards

3 projects accepted at the San Francisco MoMA Art, Architecture &
Design Collection, ADC New York, German Multimedia Award, One
Show Interactive, I.D. Magazine Award, Clio Awards New York, Graz
Biennale, London International Advertising Award, etc.

Clients

Adidas, NIVEA, Labello, Danone, Evian, Duckstein, NOAH Menschen
für Tiere, VARTA, SBT - SKIN BIOLOGY THERAPY, SportScheck,
Transmediale04, Venice Beach, etc.

FORSMAN & BODENFORS
<SWEDEN>
www.fb.se

Concept Forsman & Bodenfors mainly develops internet productions as a part of integrated advertising campaigns. We see the internet as a way to communicate a brand or a message by an entertaining interactive experience in both motion and sound. //// Forsman & Bodenfors développe principalement des productions Internet s'inscrivant dans des campagnes publicitaires intégrées. Nous concevons l'Internet comme une manière de communiquer une marque ou un message à l'aide d'une expérience sonore et animée divertissante et interactive. //// Forsman & Bodenfors erstellt hauptsächlich Internetproduktionen als Teil intergrierter Werbekampagnen. Wir sehen das Internet als ein Medium, das uns erlaubt, Produkte oder Nachrichten auf eine unterhaltsame, interaktive Weise durch Bewegung sowie Ton zu vermitteln.

http://demo.fb.se/e/kalles/site/default.asp

Name Forsman & Bodenfors

Founded 1986

Team 2 Art Directors, 2 Copywriters, 1 Agency Producer, 1 Designer, 2 Programmers, 2 Animation Artists, 1 Sound Engineer, and 1 Movie Editor.

Tools Adobe Photoshop, Adobe Illustrator, Macromedia Flash, Adobe After Effects, and Maya.

Location

Kyrkogatan 48
SE-411 08 Gothenburg
Sweden

Contact

info@fb.se

Awards

Cannes: Gold/Silver/Bronze (various), Clio Awards: Gold/Silver/
Bronze (various), Cresta Awards: Gold (various), D&AD Annual Merit
(various), Epica Awards: Gold (various), The Golden Egg: Gold/Silver
(various), Eurobest: Grand Prix/Gold/Bronze (various), New York
Festivals: Grand Award/Gold/Silver/Bronze, etc.

Clients

Volvo Cars Nordic, IKEA Sweden, Tele2Comviq, JC (Jeans & Clothes),
SCA Hygiene Products, AMF Pension, IF Insurance, Statoil,
Göteborgs-Posten, Systembolaget, Abba Seafood, Arla Foods, SVT
(Swedish Public Service Television), Wasabröd AB, etc.

FOURPAWS

‹AUSTRALIA›
www.4pd.com.au

Concept

Fourpaws Design is a web design & development company based in Melbourne, Australia. Our aim is to deliver good value, high quality web development services to small to medium size business. //// Fourpaws Design est une entreprise australienne de design et développement Internet basée à Melbourne. Nous sommes spécialisés dans l'offre de services de développement Web haute qualité aux petites et moyennes entreprises. //// Fourpaws Design ist eine Webdesign- und Produktionsgesellschaft mit Sitz in Melbourne, Australien. Unser Ziel ist es, einen wertvollen und hochqualifizierten Webseiten-Service für kleine oder mittelgrosse Firmen anzubieten.

www.beaware.org.au

Name
Fourpaws Design

Founded
2000

Team
1 Business Development Manager, 1 Project Director, 1 Art Director, 1 Designer, and 2 Developers.

Tools
Macromedia Freehand, Homesite, Macromedia Fireworks, Macromedia Flash, etc.

80 • BEST STUDIOS

Awards | Location

Unit 5/118 Miller Street
Fitzroy North, Victoria 3068
Australia

Contact

info@4pd.com.au

www.webdesigners.net.au: Site of the day (various),
www.designersdepot.com: Site of the day (various),
www.visualdesigner.net: Site of the day (various),
www.designfirms.org: Site of the day (various), etc.

Clients

Babyco, Optus, Jims Group, Wastepro, EPA, Freestone Transport,
Cameron Construction, Clement Stone, etc.

FRONT

<NORTHERN IRELAND>

www.designbyfront.com

FRONT

Concept

WE'RE NOT AFRAID TO USE PINK! Why? Because we believe the web should be original and inspirational, which is why we specialise in the design and development of websites and applications that end users enjoy using. We also like to make it easier for clients to take control without the need for technical expertise. //// UTILISER DU ROSE NE NOUS FAIT PAS PEUR ! Pourquoi ? Parce que nous pensons que le Web doit être original et inspiré. Nous sommes donc spécialisés dans la conception et le développement de sites Web et d'applications que les utilisateurs finaux prennent plaisir à utiliser. Nous aimons également faciliter la prise de contrôle de nos clients sans l'aide de spécialistes. //// Wir haben keine Angst davor, PINK zu benutzen! Warum? Weil wir denken, das Web sollte originell und inspirierend sein. Deshalb spezialisieren wir uns darin, Design und Entwicklung einer Webseite und deren Anwendung so zu gestalten, dass der Benutzer Spass dabei hat. Ausserdem sind wir darauf bedacht, es dem Kunden einfach zu machen, so dass er ohne technische Hilfe zurechtkommt.

patton.co.uk

Name FRONT

Founded 2000

Team 1 Operation/Sales, 1 Creative Director, 2 Designers, 1 Flash Developer, and 2 Backend Developers.

Tools Macromedia Flash! For developing intelligent XML based sites entirely based on AS2. Also rest of Macromedia Studio MX 2004, with our flash content management system, Crossfire, running on php/MySQL on Apache.

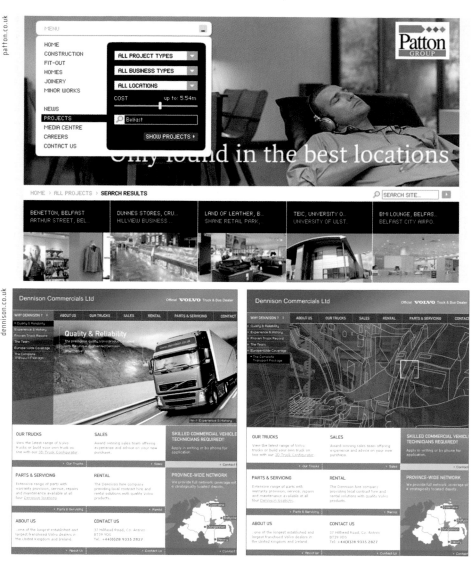

Location Alexander House, 17a Ormeau Avenue
Belfast, BT2 8HD
Northern Ireland

Contact hello@designbyfront.com

Awards Internet TINY Awards (Featured), Favourite Website Awards, Fcuk
Star Award, Shift Magazine, Linkdup, Pixelsurgeon, Moluv, Netdiver,
Design is Kinky, Well Vetted, Best Flash Animation Site, Best of
British, Digital Abstracts, Newstoday, Mixinvisuals, Crossmind,
xygoxen, Wow factor, Black is Good, Applestudios, etc.

Clients Coca Cola, Lagan Holdings, Patton Group, Northern Ireland Museums
Council, RPS Kirk McClure Morton, Hampton Conservatories, Avalon
Instruments, Dennison Commercials, etc.

FRONTMEDIA

<UK>

www.frontmedia.com

Concept

Designed for browsing devices. Simple, original, functional and effective. //// Conçu pour les dispositifs de navigation. Simple, original, fonctionnel et efficace. //// Designt für Suchmaschinen. Einfach, originell, funktional und effektiv.

www.flamingo-international.com

Name Frontmedia

Founded 1998

Team 1 Designer/Programmer, 1 Databases/Programmer and 1 Account Manager.

Tools Adobe Photoshop, Adobe Illustrator. Macromedia Flash, Macromedia Coldfusion, Macromedia Fireworks, Macromedia Freehand, Macromedia Dreamweaver, generaland relevant: pens, pencils, paper, and a scanner.

Location

15 Augustus Way
Witham, Essex CM8 1HH
United Kingdom

Contact

david@frontmedia.co.uk

Awards

Front Media has received various WebAwards and has been featured in publications such as Books: "Redesigning Websites" - Rockport Publishing, "Taschen's 1000 Favourite Websites" - Taschen, Web Designing (Japan), Web Creators (Japan), Create Online (UK), Internet (UK), Internet Works (UK), etc.

Clients

Completed projects third-party for various digital marketing agencies, includes: BP, Cisco Systems, Citroën, Harley Davidson, Mercury, and Universal Records. Direct clients include: Abbey National, Aveva Engineering IT, Flamingo International, DW Windsor Lighting, Harcourt Publishing, Higgins Homes, Higgins City, etc.

GLUE LONDON
‹UK›
www.gluelondon.com

Concept

Glue is an advertising agency. We do all the things you would expect of any reputable ad agency such as great creative, intelligent thinking and efficient service. Our main difference is that we focus purely on digital. Why only digital? Two reasons really. First, it's what we're particularly good at and second if the whole world is going digital then it seems to us like the perfect place to be. //// Glue est une agence publicitaire. Nous offrons les prestations qu'on attend de toute agence publicitaire réputée et notamment des services créatifs, intelligents et efficaces. Ce qui fait notre différence, c'est principalement que nous sommes orientés uniquement vers le numérique. Pourquoi ? Il y a deux raisons à cela. D'abord parce que c'est un domaine où nous excellons particulièrement. Ensuite parce que le monde entier empruntant la voie du numérique, il nous semble que c'est l'endroit où il faut être aujourd'hui. //// Glue ist eine Werbeagentur. Wir bieten all das, was Sie von einer kompetenten Werbeagentur erwarten, so wie hervorragende Kreativität, intelligentes Denken und einen effizienten Service. Unser Hauptmerkmal ist, dass wir ausschliesslich auf digitale Arbeitsvorgänge spezialisiert sind. Warum nur digital? Es gibt zwei Gründe dafür: Erstens, wir sind besonders gut darin und zweitens, nachdem sich die ganze Welt auf digital umstellt, glauben auch wir, dass darin die Zukunft liegt.

www.naturalnoodling.com

Name glue London

Founded 1999

Team 1 Creative Director, 3 Art Directors, 3 Copywriters, 1 Head of Art, 2 Design Directors, 2 Senior Designers, 2 Designers, 3 Illustrators, 1 Rich Media Developer, 4 Developers, 1 Production Director, 3 Producers, 1 Planning Director, 3 Planners, 11 Professionals in Account Management positions, and 7 Management positions.

Tools Macromedia Flash, Wildform Flix, Sorenson Squeeze, Adobe Photoshop/Imageready, Adobe Illustrator, Adobe After Effects, Apple Final Cut Express, Apple iMovie, Steinberg Cubase SX3, Apple DVD Studio Pro 2, Visual Studio, Quicktime Pro, Actionscript, .Net, XML, php 5 and hardcore Javascript, C#, SOAP, etc.

www.euro2004.t-mobile.co.uk/index_dev.php

www.naturalnoodling.com

Location

31-39 Redchurch Street
London, E2 7DJ
United Kingdom

Contact

hello@gluelondon.com

Awards

Cannes Lions: Gold/Bronze (various), MSN Gallery: Winner (Grand
Prix, FMCG, etc), GRAMIA Awards (Silver), IAB Creative Showcase
(Winner), London International Advertising Awards (Gold),
Interactive Marketing and Advertising Awards: Winner (Interactive
Media, Finance, Agency of the Year and Rich Media), etc.

Clients

T-Mobile, Virgin (Atlantic, Trains, Money), McDonald's, Unilever
(Pot Noodle, Impulse), Associated New Media, Sky, Mazda, McCain's,
Masterfoods, COI (Royal Marines, Royal Navy, Inland Revenue), MTV,
Nokia and Royal Sun, Alliance, etc.

GOLPEAVISA!

<MEXICO>

www.golpeavisa.com.mx

Concept

Golpeavisa it's a proudly Mexican design studio which projects are made with more love than technique. //// Nous sommes un studio mexicain de design. Nous mettons beaucoup d'amour (bien plus que de technique) dans les projets qui nous sont confiés. //// Golpeavisa ist ein stolzes, mexikanisches Designstudio, dessen Projekte mit mehr Liebe als Technik entstehen.

www.golpeavisa.com.mx/adidas.html

Name: Golpeavisa!

Founded: 2002

Team: 2 Graphic/Flash Designers/Illustrators, and 1 Graphic Designer.

Tools: Macromedia Flash, Adobe Illustrator, and Adobe Photoshop.

Location

Valle del Cedro # 32 Izcalli del Valle
Tultitlan Edo. de Mex. CP 54945
Mexico

Contact

eldiablo@golpeavisa.com.mx

Awards

FLAvorito, Inspirational Latin Site, Web Award: Award of Excellence
(various), etc.

Clients

'El Solecito' (Weekly suplement for kids of 'El Sol de México'
newspaper), Altavista Graphics (Printing Company in Chicago, IL),
Adidas, etc.

GRANATTA

\<SPAIN\>

www.granatta.com

Concept

Our main motto is something we use to call "simplejidad" (simplicity), on how we use our skills for developing both websites and applications with a solid and subtle interactive-backend programming and, at the same time, very easy-to-use and update. //// Notre principale devise est ce que nous avons coutume d'appeler "simplejidad" (simplicité). Simplicité dans notre manière d'utiliser nos compétences pour développer des sites Web et des applications à l'aide d'une programmation backend interactive subtile et solide à la fois mais aussi très facile à utiliser et à mettre à jour. //// Unser Motto ist "simplejidad" (Vereinfachung) in Bezug darauf, wie wir unsere Fähigkeiten dazu einsetzen, Webseiten sowie Anwendungen mit einem soliden und gut strukturierten interaktivem Programm zu konstruieren, die gleichzeitig einfach für update und Benutzung sind.

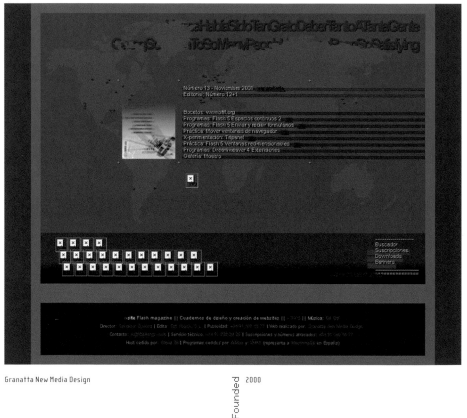

Name Granatta New Media Design

Founded 2000

Team 1 Art Director, 1 Interactive Designer, and 1 Backend Programmer.

Tools Macromedia Flash

05. campanasVela
sonido actualmente detenido

¡Arráncame del suelo!... cosas ilógicas, cosas inestables, saltarines al ralentí... media hora en el aire.

La Radio ⊗   instrucciones

Aunque Val del Omar citara frecuentemente que la línea más corta entre dos puntos tiene forma de curva, La Radio ⊗ se compone de puntos y líneas rectas que los unen, siendo los cruces entre dichas líneas los que generan al pulsarse las distintas frecuencias en las que se emiten contenidos, pero ¡alerta! no es sueño la vida ni todo lo que se escucha tiene por qué estar correctamente sintonizado. Desplaza los puntos extremos de cada recta para generar puntos de corte entre ellas y encontrar un lugar desde el que la recepción sea idónea; cuantas más ⊗ consigas formar con las rectas mayor número de frecuencias tendrás disponibles en esta nuestra Radio ⊗ y recuerda que puedes eliminar cada sonido eliminando el punto de corte que lo genera.

PS: La existencia de esta pieza se debe al proyecto editado por Bípodos y Dígitos que conmemoran el décimo ⊗ aniversario de la edición del último número de la revista Fíjate. Los elementos gráficos aquí utilizados corresponden a la imaginación de Leo, cuya creatividad alcanzó su temperatura de fusión mientras diseñaba pegatinas para plotear en vinilo con objeto de llenar las calles de ⊗ :-)

La Radio ⊗   créditos

Sol Diurno
Ilumina la Alhambra durante la noche

Sol Nocturno
Ilumina la Alhambra durante el día

Lámpara Mágica
Proporciona extractos del universo de José Val del Omar cuando se frota con mimo

"El que ama arde, y el que arde vuela a la velocidad de la luz"

Dani Granatta
www.granatta.com

Hacedor táctil

Ángel Arias
www.gran-nada.com

Bicho bioelectrónico

Martes, 22 de Abril de 2003 — Carmen Heras se reúne con empresarios y vecinos
Jueves, 24 de Abril de 2003 — Presentación de candidatura
Viernes, 25 de Abril de 2003 — Proyecto integral de tráfico y obras

otra forma de ser, otra forma de actuar
Carmen Heras
CANDIDATA A LA ALCALDÍA DE CÁCERES

PSOE   La candidata | Opiniones | El programa | Entrevista | Contacta | Más noticias

Jueves, 1 de Agosto de 2002 — Denuncia sobre el gerente del Plan Urban
Sábado, 3 de Agosto de 2002 — Heras rechaza las acusaciones de demagogia
Miércoles, 18 de Septiembre de 200 — Inexistencia de bibliotecas en barrios

Foto oficial de la candidatura del PSOE a las Elecciones Municipales de 2003 tomada en la subida al Santuario de la Montaña

PSOE   La candidata | Opiniones | El programa | Entrevista | Contacto | La campaña

Location

Gómez Becerra 18 4,
CP 10001, Cáceres
Spain

Contact

null@granatta.com

Awards

Macromedia Spain Site of the Week (various), Flash Film Festival Barcelona: Best Interactive Piece Online, Flash Film Festival Barcelona: Finalist for Best Documentary Piece Online, Möbius Barcelona Multimedia Awards: Best Net-Art Application, etc.

Clients

BBVA, Anaya Multimedia, Linex.org, Furuno, PSOE, Diputación de Zaragoza, Instituto de Artes Visuales, etc.

GROUP94

\<BELGIUM\>

www.group94.com

Concept

Group94 produces advanced solutions for the web with much attention for detail and originality and most dedicated to functionality and usability. Most of our clients are related to design or creativity in a way or another: agency's, photographers, artists, architects, museums, musicians, etc… //// Group94 produit des solutions avancées pour le Web. Des solutions dans lesquelles s'expriment un sens aigu du détail et une grande originalité et qui sont principalement tournées vers la fonctionnalité et la convivialité. La plupart de nos clients ont d'une manière ou une autre des affinités avec le design ou la créativité : il s'agit en effet d'agences, de photographes, d'artistes, d'architectes, de musées, de musiciens, etc… //// Group94 bietet fortgeschrittene Lösungen fürs Web, wobei wir unseren Schwerpunkt auf Detailtreue, Originalität sowie Funktionalität und Gebrauchsfähigkeit legen. Die meisten unserer Kunden haben auf die eine oder andere Weise mit Design oder Kreativität zu tun: Agenturen, Fotografen, Künstler, Museen, Musiker etc…

www.ourtype.com

Name group94

Founded 2000

Team 1 Creative Director, 1 Project Manager, 2 Designers, and 2 Programmers.

Tools Macromedia Flash, xhtml, XML, and php.

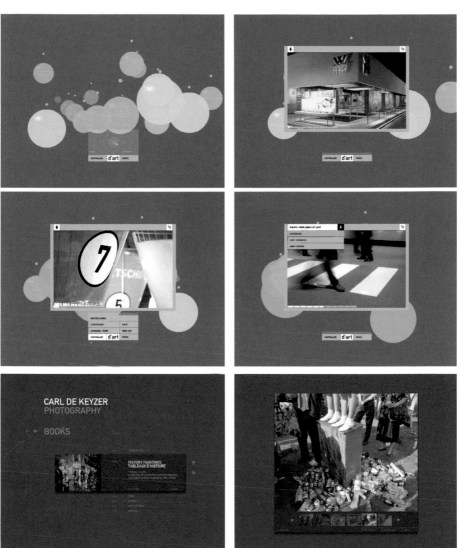

CARL DE KEYZER
PHOTOGRAPHY

←· BOOKS

Location

Guldenspoorstraat 21
9000 Gent
Belgium

Contact

info@group94.com

Awards

FWA: Site of the Day/Site of the Month, QBN Certified/NewsToday,
FlashForward (finalist), Flashkit, Netdiver, AmericanDesingAwards,
BombShockAward, BestFlashAnimationSite, WellVetted,
Cannes Cyber (nominee), Internet TinyAwards, DesignTaxi.com,
VisuelOrgasm Top 20, etc.

Clients

Marge Casey + Associates, D'Art Design Gruppe, Carl De Keyer, Push
Advertising Agency, Balé Port Douglas, OurType, StratoCucine,
Royal Botania, Dirk Lambrechts Photography, Kollektief Interior
Architecture, Ghent Fine Arts Museum, Gigue Fashion, Verne
Photography, City of Kortrijk, Ozark Henry, etc.

GRUPO W

<MEXICO>

www.grupow.com

Concept

We like to think we are a factory of experiences. The work we do has a personal signature of our artists, developers, and producers. We think in users shocked by a web site, and we like to involve them in a complete mood with great graphic designs, awesome sound production, animation with life, and all these elements in a global sensation. All an experience. //// Nous aimons nous considérer comme une usine à expériences. Les travaux que nous fournissons portent la signature de nos artistes, développeurs et producteurs. Nous pensons que les utilisateurs doivent éprouver un choc en découvrant un site Web et aimons faire pénétrer les internautes dans une ambiance faite de formidables graphismes, d'un son redoutable et d'animations vivantes, tous ces éléments devant former une sensation globale. Toute une expérience. //// **Wir beschreiben uns gerne als eine Fabrik von Erfahrungen. Die Arbeiten, die wir erstellen, tragen die persönliche Unterschrift unserer Künstler, Produzenten sowie Hersteller. Wir stellen uns Verbraucher vor, die von einer Webseite geschockt sind und möchten sie in eine Stimmung mitnehmen, voller faszinierender Grafikdesigns, genialer Soundproduktionen sowie Animation. Eine komplette Sensation und ganz besondere Erfahrung.**

www.grupow.com/bimbo/juego

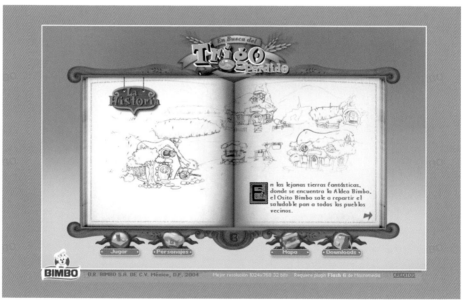

Name	GRUPO W	Founded	1999

Team

Production Director, Creative Director, Art Director, Illustrator Senior, Web Master, Action Script Programer, Administrative Contact (one person of each cathegory above), and 3 Senior Designers.

Tools

Macromedia Flash, Corel Fractal Painter, Macromedia Dreamweaver, Adobe Premiere, Adobe Audition, Adobe After Effects, Discreet 3D Studio Max, etc.

Paseo de las Gardenias 395, Parques de la Canada,
Saltillo, Coahuila, CP 25000
Mexico

uvalencia@grupow.com

Círculo Creativo Mexico (various), Premio internacional al
diseño (Featured), One Show Interactive: Gold/Silver (various),
Flashformexico, How Design Magazine, FIAP, Ojo de Iberoamérica
(Gold), Wow-factor-Featured site, Pleasezine (Featured), FlashKit,
iBest Award-best interactive agency of Mexico, etc.

Comex, Bimbo, GMAC Latin america, HSBC Mexico, FCB Mexico, etc.

HEAVYFORM

<SERBIA AND MONTENEGRO>

www.heavyform.com

Concept

Heavyform diverges from others. Capable of various forms, it's made out of distinct characteristics, qualities, and elements. Mission is to explore new ways of expressing interactive design combining as much tools as possible. It's a place for promotion of our work, a portfolio site. //// Heavyform n'est pas un site comme les autres. Pouvant prendre des formes diverses, il est constitué de caractéristiques, qualités et éléments différents. Sa mission est d'explorer de nouvelles manières de faire du design interactif en combinant le plus d'outils possible. Il s'agit d'un lieu de promotion de notre travail, un site portfolio. //// Heavyform unterscheidet sich von allen anderen. Wir besitzen bestimmte Charakteristiken, Qualitäten und Elemente sowie die Fähigkeit, verschiedene Formen anzunehmen. Das Ziel ist es, neue Ausdrucksformen für interaktives Design zu finden und dabei so viele Hilfsmittel und Werkzeuge wie möglich zu nutzen. Hier stellen wir unsere Arbeit zur Schau, eine Portfolio-Seite.

www.heavyform.com

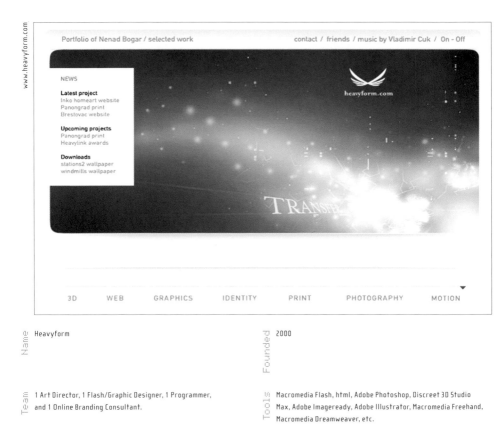

Name Heavyform

Founded 2000

Team 1 Art Director, 1 Flash/Graphic Designer, 1 Programmer, and 1 Online Branding Consultant.

Tools Macromedia Flash, html, Adobe Photoshop, Discreet 3D Studio Max, Adobe Imageready, Adobe Illustrator, Macromedia Freehand, Macromedia Dreamweaver, etc.

Location

Lifke Sandora 11
24000 Subotica
Serbia and Montenegro

Contact

nenad@heavyform.com

Awards

American design awards, Plasticpilots 3 Star Awarded Webiste, DOPE, Kirupa, Organicpixel, King for a week: finalist (various), Designersnetwork, Arttech festival of digital arts, Xpose festival of digital arts, etc. Also fearuted at Linkdup, Styleboost, Newwebpick, Moluv, etc.

Clients

CukMediaGroup, INKO Homeart, Flohmani, Extel, Digiplates, Urbancolo, Applocker, Fratellis, Malcon d.o.o, Brestovac d.o.o, Propaganda creative team, Sewdown, Bonaparte art magazine, Panongrad, TopTip realestates, Projekt gradnja d.o.o, GtI computers, etc.

HELIOS

\<CANADA\>

www.heliozilla.com

Dirty but sexy. //// Indécent mais sexy. //// Schmutzig, aber sexy.

www.giantscreenbugs.com

Name	Helios Design Laboratories	Founded 1990
Team	6 Designers with multi-disciplinary skills, and an army of Freelancers.	Tools Humour, etc.

Location

489 Queen Street West, 4th floor
Toronto, Ontario, M5V 2B4
Canada

Contact

hello@heliozilla.com

Awards

Applied Arts Annual: Gold (various), Communication Arts: Award of Excellence (various), Juno Awards, and Springfield Elementary School: Perfect Attendance Award.

Clients

Adobe, Arnold Advertising, Bertelsman, Decode, Dreamworks, Epic, Fuse TV, Geffen, K2 Snowboards, Leo Burnett, Lowe Roche, Mclaren McCann, Miramax/Rolling Thunder, Natrel, Nike, OK47, Royal Bank of Canada , Sony Music, Temple Street, TBWA Chiat Day, Universal Music, Vice Magazine, Virgin Music, Warner Music, etc.

HI-RES!

‹UK›

www.hi-res.net

HiRes!

Concept Handsome information - Radical entertainment Systems! //// Superbes données, des systèmes de divertissement radicaux ! //// Hübsch verpackte Information - radikales Unterhaltungssystem!

www.the-dreamers.com

Name Hi-ReS!

Founded 1999

Team 2 Creative/Artistic Directors, 2 Designer, 1 Programmer, 1 Rich Media Developer, plus a pool of talented Freelancers to expand the team on demand.

Tools Pencil and paper, Macromedia Flash, Adobe Photoshop, digital camera, etc.

Location

8-9 Rivington Place
London EC2A 3BA
United Kingdom

Contact

info@hi-res.net

Awards

Cannes Lions: Gold Cyberlion (various), Clio Awards Internet
Advertising (Gold), Oneshow Interactive: Gold Winner (various),
London International Advertising Awards (various), Prix Ars
Electronica, BAFTA (British Academy of Film and Television Arts),
Flash Film Festival San Francisco, Art Directors Club New York, etc.

Clients

HBO, Artisan Entertainment, Lionsgate Films, New Market Films,
Fox Searchlight, NTT Data, AOL Advertising Promotion INC, Dentsu,
TBWA\London, Wieden + Kennedy, Mitsubishi Motors, Lexus Motors,
Sony Computer Entertainment, The Coca-Cola Company, Christian
Aid, EMI Records, Virgin Records, Sony Music, Diesel Clothing, etc.

HUGE

<USA>

www.hugeinc.com

We make it special. //// Nous faisons de tout quelque chose de spécial. //// Wir machen etwas ganz besonderes.

www.atlanticrecords.com

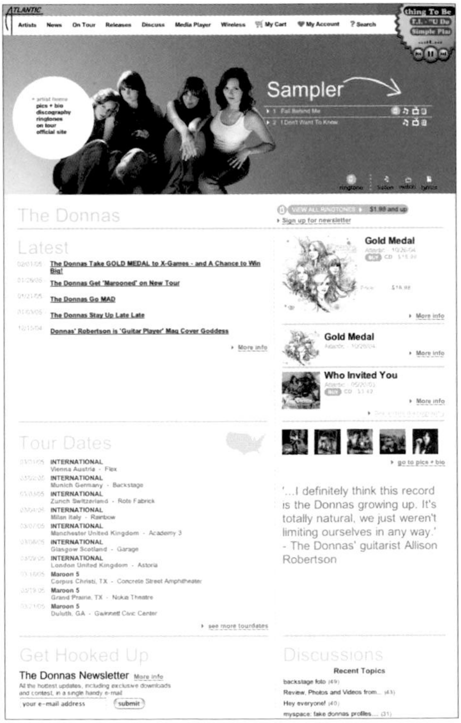

Name HUGE

Founded 1999

Team Directors of Production, Strategic Planning, Account Services, Interaction Design; Account Managers, Project Managers, Designers, Web Developers/Programmers, Flash Developers, Interaction Designers, Information Architects, Usability Analysts, Illustrators, Creative Director, and Production artists.

Tools Macromedia Flash, Adobe Photoshop, Adobe Illustrator, Macromedia Dreamweaver, PHP/ASP/JSP, MySQL, Stictly valid html/CSS, Javascript, Actionscript 1.0 / 2.0, XML, etc.

Location

20 Jay Street 10th Floor
Brooklyn, NY 11201
USA

Contact

dksokna@hugeinc.com

Awards

Communication Arts Website of the Week, Entablature's
Architecture Web Site Awards (Gold), E-project,
Favourite Website Awards (various), Web Design Magazine,
Tendenze Dinamiche Del Web, etc.

Clients

AOL, Atlantic Records, Bad Boy Records, Brooklyn Chamber of
Commerce, CNBC, Conde Nast, Hillier Architects, Hunter College,
IKEA, IPC Information Systems, New Line Cinema, Normandy
Ventures, OneCare, PalTalk, Primaris Airlines, Silverpop Systems,
Style.com, Vogue.com, Universal/Motown Record Group, etc.

ITCAT MEDIA
\<HONG KONG\>
www.itcatmedia.com

itCat Media

Concept

ItCat Media aims to provide strategic, creative, and media services that help clients meet and exceed their online business goal. //// ItCat Media propose des services créatifs et stratégiques visant à aider ses clients à atteindre et dépasser leur objectif commercial en ligne. //// ItCat Media zielt darauf ab, einen strategischen und kreativen Medienservice zu bieten, um somit Kunden zu helfen, ihre Geschäftsziele online zu erreichen und sogar zu übertreffen.

www.itcatmedia.com

Name ItCat Media Limited

Founded 2000

Team 1 Creative Director, 1 Art Directors, 2 Designer, 1 Account Manger, 2 Account Executive, and 1 Business Development Manager.

Tools Adobe Photoshop, Adobe Illustrator, Macromedia Flash, Macromedia Dreamweaver, Macromedia Fireworks, etc.

Location Accommodation Restaurants & Lounges Meetings Recreation About Us

NEWS Loading..

2002 Conrad Hong Kong All Rights Reserved

Privacy Policy

Location

1902, Chung Nam Building,
1 Lockhart Road, Wan Chai
Hong Kong

Contact

stephen@itcatmedia.com

Awards

MerComm iNova (Winner), SXSW Awards (Winner), IDN Magazine
Design Contest (People's Choice Awards), Macromedia Asia Spotlight
Gallery, Flashkit.com Site of the day, etc.

Clients

AT&T, Conrad Hotel, Novartis, Sony, Samsung, Canon, Medecins
Sans Frontiers, etc.

KINETIC

<SINGAPORE>
www.kinetic.com.sg

Concept

"How the hell did they do that?" Benjy Choo – "Great Scotts... ITS ALIVE!!... well sort of anyway..." Sean Lam //// "C'est incroyable, je ne sais pas comment ils ont fait pour arriver à un tel résultat ?" Benjy Choo – "Sacrés Ecossais... L'ECRAN VIT !! (enfin, presque)" Sean Lam //// "Wie zum Teufel haben sie das hingekriegt?" Benjui Choo – "Grossartige Scotts....Es lebt!!....naja, zumindest sowas ähnliches..." Sean Lam

www.grouplotus.com

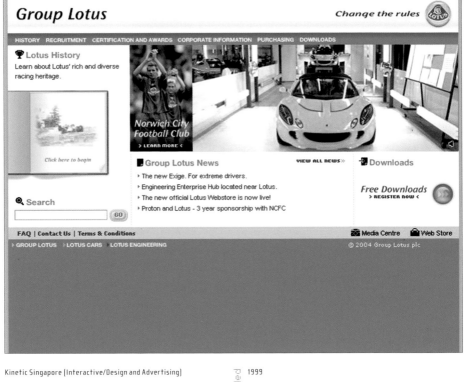

Name: Kinetic Singapore (Interactive/Design and Advertising)

Founded: 1999

Team: 2 Art Directors, and 3 Flash Designers.

Tools: Macromedia Flash, Macromedia Dreamweaver, Adobe Photoshop, Audition, etc.

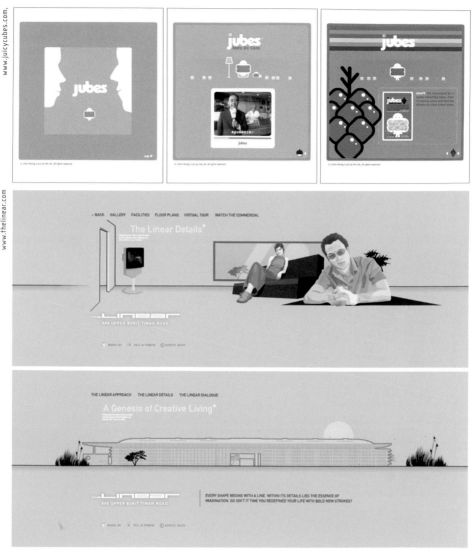

Location 2 Leng Kee Road,
Thye Hong Centre, #04-03A, 159086
Singapore

Contact carolyn@kinetic.com.sg

Awards Singapore Creative Circle Awards, One Show Interactive, Clio
Awards, Young Guns Awards, Communication Arts Interactive Annual
Magazine Entry, New York Festival, etc.

Clients Aamer Taher Design, Amara Holdings, Heineken, Cathay, Citibank,
FHM, Ho Bee, Iteru.net, Lorgans, Lotus, Motorola Electronics,
Hongkong Shanghai Bank, Nokia, Pestbusters, Public Utilities Board,
Shell, Shooting Gallery Asia, Singapore Telecommunications, Six
Planes, StarHub, Yellow Box Studios, Yahoo Asia, etc.

KLEBER

\<UK\>

www.kleber.net

Concept Innovative user-centric design: Kleber's forte has always been a clear balance between aesthetics and functionality. //// Design innovant centré sur l'utilisateur : le point fort de Kleber a toujours été l'équilibre entre l'esthétique et la fonctionnalité. //// Innovatives verbrauchergerechtes Design: Klebers Stärke war schon immer eine klare Balance zwischen Ästhetik und Funktionalität.

www.bleep.com

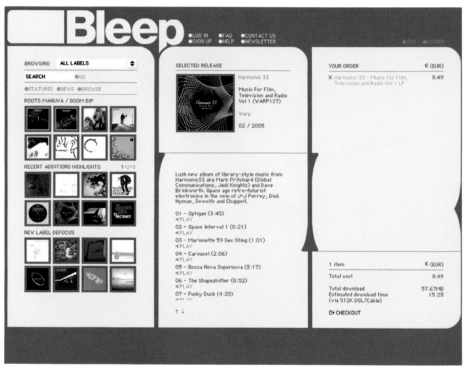

Name Kleber Design Ltd.

Founded 1996

Team 2 Creative Directors, and 1 Technical Director.

Tools Adobe Photoshop, html, xhtml, XML, PHP/MySQL, Macromedia Flash, etc.

Awards

DMA, IMA, NME Net Sounds, DMAs (various), CADs, etc.

Location

3rd Floor, 95A Rivington Street
EC2A 3AY London
United Kingdom

Contact

yes@kleber.net

Clients

The Beatles, The Designers Republic, The Echo Label, Parlophone,
EMI Music, FatCat Records, Head Heritage, Hydrogen Jukebox,
Manhattan Loft Corporation, MTV Networks Europe, Ninja Tune,
Peacefrog Records, Pressure Sounds, Sioux Records, Sony BMG
Music, Universal Everything, Warp Records, etc.

KNOWAWALL

<USA>

www.knowawall.com

Concept — Knowawall Design creates refined interactive media that is both intuitive and engaging. //// Knowawall Design crée des médias interactifs sophistiqués à la fois intuitifs et intéressants. //// Knowawall Design kreiert hochentwickelte interaktive Medien, die sowohl intuitiv als auch einnehmend sind.

www.knowawall.com

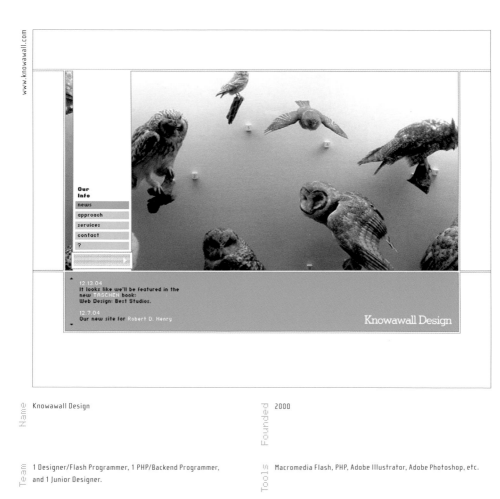

Name — Knowawall Design

Founded — 2000

Team — 1 Designer/Flash Programmer, 1 PHP/Backend Programmer, and 1 Junior Designer.

Tools — Macromedia Flash, PHP, Adobe Illustrator, Adobe Photoshop, etc.

Location

428 Broadway, #35
New York, NY 10013
USA

Contact

hello@knowawall.com

Awards

FWA [various] and Internet Tiny Award.

Clients

Stephen Yablon Architect, Hut Sachs Studio, Robert D. Henry
Architects, Nitin Vadukul Studio, Vik Muniz, Misha Gravenor,
Control Group, Yrmis, Jaap Buitendijk, Dan Silvertree, Bryce
Wolkowitz Gallery, etc.

LES CHINOIS

‹FRANCE›

www.leschinois.com

Concept

All this work just to be able to play at the office. //// Tout ce boulot rien que pour pouvoir jouer au bureau. //// Diese ganze Arbeit, nur um im Büro spielen zu können.

www.leschinois.com

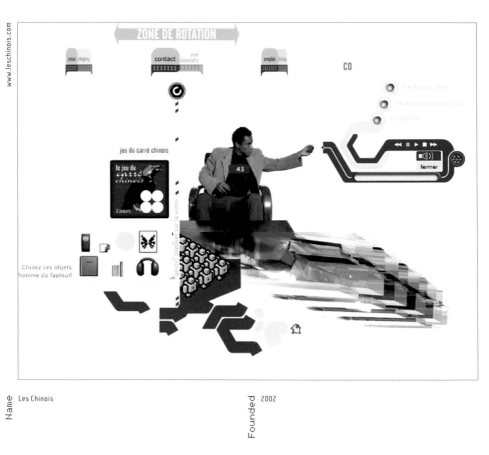

Name Les Chinois

Founded 2002

Team 2 Art Directors, 2 Web Designers, 6 Developers, 1 Project Manager, and 1 Sales Manager.

Tools Macromedia Flash, Adobe Photoshop, Adobe Illustrator, Adobe After Effects, Adobe Premiere, Discreet 3D Studio Max, etc.

www.lexon-design.com

Location Pépinière Paris Cyber Village, 101-103
Bd Mac Donald
75019 Paris
France

Awards Macromedia, FWA, Club des AD, Moluv, Turkeyawarsd, Flashxpress,
Télérama, Praktica, etc.

Contact contact@leschinois.com

Clients Audi, Adidas, Waterman, Société Générale, Dassault Systemes, M6,
Daddy, Lexon, etc.

LOST BOYS

<THE NETHERLANDS>

www.lostboys.nl

Concept
Lost Boys provides interactive communication, campaigning and client services. Creative and effective since 1993. //// Lost Boys propose des services interactifs client, de campagne publicitaire et de communication. Créatif et efficace depuis 1993. //// Lost Boys bietet interaktive Kommunikation, Werbung und Kundenservice. Kreativ und effektiv seit 1993.

www.vaya.nl

Name Lost Boys

Founded 1993

Team 3 Strategists, 9 Art Directors, 1 Copy Writer, 1 Usability Director, 6 Interaction Designers, 5 Flash Action Scripters, 5 .net Developers, 13 Java Developers, 5 Front-end Developers, 2 Tridion Developers, 5 Technical Consultants, and 12 Project Managers.

Tools Tridion, Macromedia Flash, dhtml, Java/open source, .Net, etc.

Location

Joop Geesinkweg 209
1096 AV Amsterdam
The Netherlands

Awards

Cannes Lion, Europrix, Spin Awards, etc.

Contact

info@lostboys.nl

Clients

Anne Frank Foundation, Nuon, KLM, Postbank, Volkswagen, Efteling, Mercedes, Mentos, Vaya, etc.

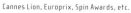

LUMEN

‹CZECH REPUBLIC›

www.lumenstudio.net

Concept
The net should be more accessible, more interesting and informative so we try to work in this direction. And it's a long distance run... ////
Le Net devrait être plus accessible, plus intéressant et plus informatif. Nous essayons de travailler en ce sens. La route est longue... //// **Das Netz**
sollte einfacher zugänglich sein, interessanter und informativer, daher bemühen wir uns, darauf hinzuarbeiten. Und wir haben noch einen
langen Weg vor uns...

www.defile.cz

Name **Lumen Design Studio**

Founded **2003**

Team **1 Art Director, 2 Programmers, 2 Coders/Flash Designers, and 4 Photographers.**

Tools **Xhtml, XML, CSS, Macromedia Flash, PHP, MySQL, Head, etc.**

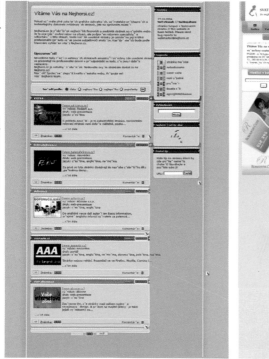

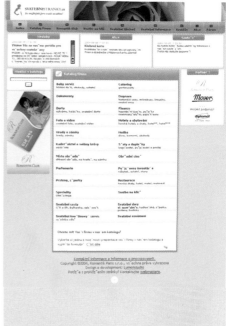

Location

Narodni trida 25
Prague
Czech Republic

Contact

info@lumenstudio.net

Awards

Fcukstar.com, Thedreamer(Brazil), 4Efx.com.br (alternative design), Newwebpick.com, Visuellerorgasmus.de, etc.

Clients

Défilé FashionBar&Lounge, Gembitec Datensicherheit, Titan Consulting Group inc, etc.

MACHBAR

\<GERMANY>
www.machbar.com

Concept

Curiosity builds the web! Machbar develops absolutely appropriate or totally surprising web solutions, from comprehensive conceptual work to top quality realization. //// *La curiosité crée le Web ! Machbar développe des solutions Web totalement appropriées ou entièrement surprenantes, allant du travail conceptuel complet à la réalisation de qualité optimale.* //// **Neugierde lässt das Web wachsen! Machbar entwickelt absolut passende oder total überraschende Weblösungen, von komplett konzeptioneller Arbeit bis hin zu Realisierungen von Top-Qualität.**

www.conma.de

VERSTEHEN WIR KOMPLEXE ZUSAMMENHÄNGE?

| | || | 1 | 2| 3 | 4 5 | 6 | || |

2.SINN: HÖREN

IMPRESSUM   FAKTEN   LEISTUNGEN   REFERENZEN   JOBS   KONTAKT

Name MACHBAR	**Founded** 1997

Team 2 Consultants, 2 Project Manager, 1 Creative Director, 1 Art Director, 2 Designers, and 3 Programmers.	**Tools** Everything that's worth working with!

Location

Königsgalerie, Treppenstraße 3 / D-34117 Kassel

Frankfurter Tor 9 / D-10243 Berlin

Germany

Contact

mail@machbar.com

Awards

Art Directors Club Germany, Best of Business Award, Red Dot Award, Macromedia Site of the week, etc.

Clients

RICOH, AGCO/Massey Ferguson, Stuttgart Stock Exchange, Bravo. de, Documenta, Scl Games Ltd, City of Kassel, Bertelsmann Group, Heinrich Bauer, GFT AG, Enowa, Gleistein Ropes, Hübner, VA Tech SAT/Vienna, KfW, etc.

MACHINAS

\<SPAIN\>

www.machinas.com

Concept

Machinas services span website planning, design, development, hosting, marketing, consulting, maintenance and analysis. Core to Machinas work is a seamless design perspective with a holistic view of the communication intention and structure for delivery - modern design, clean clear visual communication and intuitive interaction. //// Les services proposés par Machinas couvrent la planification, la conception, le développement, l'hébergement, le marketing, le consulting, la maintenance et l'analyse de sites Web. Au centre du travail de Machinas se trouve une perspective de conception continue associée à une vision holistique de l'intention de communication et de la structure proposée : design moderne, communication visuelle claire et interactions intuitives. //// Der Machinas Service umfasst Planung, Design, Entwicklung, Hosting, Marketing, Wartung, Analyse und Beratung für Webseiten. Im Mittelpunkt der Machinas Arbeiten steht nahtloses, modernes Design, mit einer ganzheitlichen, klaren visuellen Kommunikation und intuitiver Handhabung.

www.machinas.com

machinas digital works

ENGLISH | DEUTSCH

ABOUT
WORKS
PROJECTS
CONTACT
JOBS
HOME

IN THE WORKS

Esprit US online store.
Esprit recently launched their new online store in the US. Machinas worked closely with Esprit to advance the design of the e*shop for the US market. A supporting online advertising campaign sees ads designed and produced by Machinas appearing on Yahoo and major shopping portals.

Multichannel websites for Sopexa.
Soon to launch is a group of three sites for the French food and drink marketing and communications specialists, Sopexa. Machinas are helping to build Sopexa's presence in Spain and Portugal.

Deus ex machina.
As a result of extensive experience building and maintaining international websites, Machinas has developed a solid understanding of the issues involved in multilingual, multicultural, multichannel, multinational sites. The DXM multilingual web content management system helps simplify all of that. Watch out for complete details coming soon.

Name Machinas

Founded 2000

Team 1 Art Director, 1 Communications Director, 3 Web/Flash Designers, 2 Developers, and 1 Account Executive.

Tools Design, Usability, Communication, Functionality, Interaction, html, CSS, XML, Macromedia Flash, PHP, .NET, ColdFusion, etc.

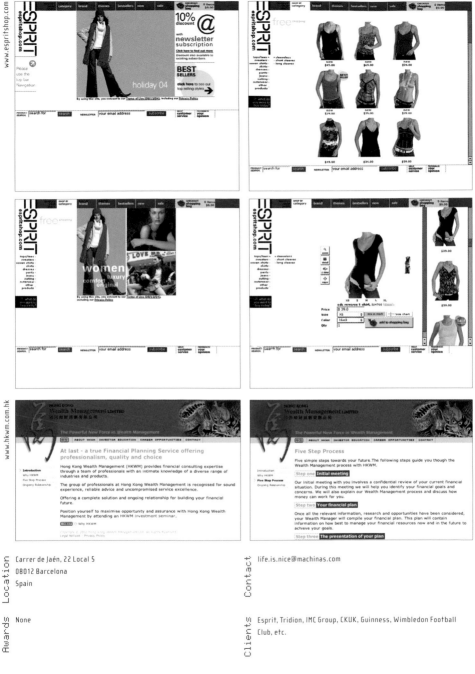

Awards   Location

Carrer de Jaén, 22 Local 5

08012 Barcelona

Spain

None

Contact

life.is.nice@machinas.com

Clients

Esprit, Tridion, IMC Group, CKUK, Guinness, Wimbledon Football Club, etc.

MATEPUANA

<RUSSIA/BELARUS>

www.matepuana.com

Concept

First long I think, then quickly I do. //// Une longue gestation suivie d'une exécution rapide. //// Zuerst denke ich lange, dann handle ich rasch.

Open! Design

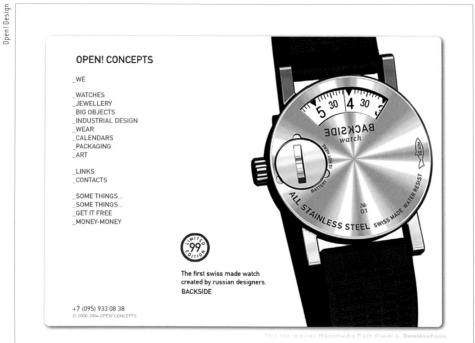

OPEN! CONCEPTS

_WE

_WATCHES
_JEWELLERY
_BIG OBJECTS
_INDUSTRIAL DESIGN
_WEAR
_CALENDARS
_PACKAGING
_ART

_LINKS
_CONTACTS

_SOME THINGS...
_SOME THINGS...
_GET IT FREE
_MONEY-MONEY

The first swiss made watch
created by russian designers.
BACKSIDE

+7 (095) 933 08 38
© 2000-2004 OPEN! CONCEPTS

This site requires Macromedia Flash Player 6. Download now.

Name Matepuana project

Founded 2000

Team One-man creative office with incorporated Freelancers
according to necessity.

Tools Macromedia Flash and brain.

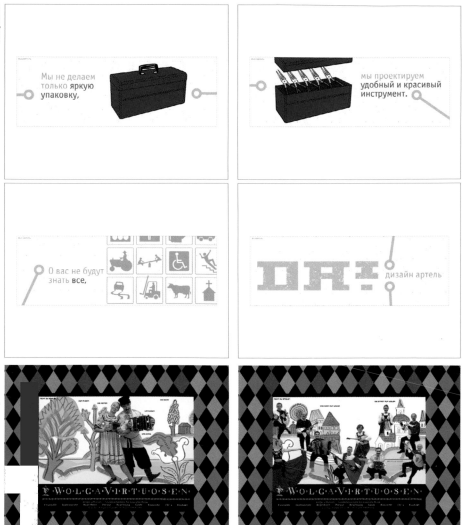

Location

Zaslavskaya str., 25, 557. Minsk
Belarus
Festivalnaya str., 22/4, 46. Moskow
Russia

Contact

mtpna@matepuana.com

Awards

Design Innovation Awards, 13th International Advertising Moscow
Festival, ARTFLASH, Golden website, Golden Wolf, etc.

Clients

OPEN!DESIGN, plenki.net, Wolga Virtuosen, U.S. Journal of
Academics, efa gruppe, Erigami, Atlant Telecom, Victor Kopach,
Rodina.by, Pixelhead, Twinbirds, Tiron America, Webmascon, Aitoc,
Design Artel, IT4Profi, Intervelopers, Christian Zimmerli, Epam
Systems, Dact, LEMT, BelOMO, Krinitsa, Jdanovichi, etc.

MAX WEBER

\<POLAND\>

www.maxweber.com

Concept

We specialize in creations of a very high visual and emotional standard. The expression of design always helps functionality and features of realized production. We work for clients and with clients. We are looking for individual and effective solutions. Our goal is to be extremely effective. //// Nous sommes spécialisés dans la création de standards extrêmement visuels et émotionnels. Le design est toujours au service de la fonctionnalité et des caractéristiques de la production réalisée. Nous travaillons pour et avec nos clients. Nous sommes à la recherche de solutions individuelles et efficaces. Notre objectif est une efficacité maximale. //// Wir sind spezialisiert auf die Kreation eines sehr hohen visuellen sowie emotionalen Standards. Der Ausdruck durch Design hilft stets bei der Funktionalität und den Merkmalen einer durchgeführten Produktion. Wir arbeiten für Kunden und mit Kunden. Wir suchen nach individuellen und effektiven Lösungen. Unser Ziel ist es, besonders effektiv zu sein.

www.tvn.pl

Name

Max Weber

Founded

2000

Team

2 Art/Creative Directors, 5 Graphic Designers, 3 Animators, 2 Flash Programmers, and 3 Web Producers.

Tools

Macromedia Flash, Macromedia Dreamweaver, Communication Server, Adobe Photoshop, Adobe Illustrator, Adobe After Effects, Firefox, Thunderbird, XML, dhtml, etc.

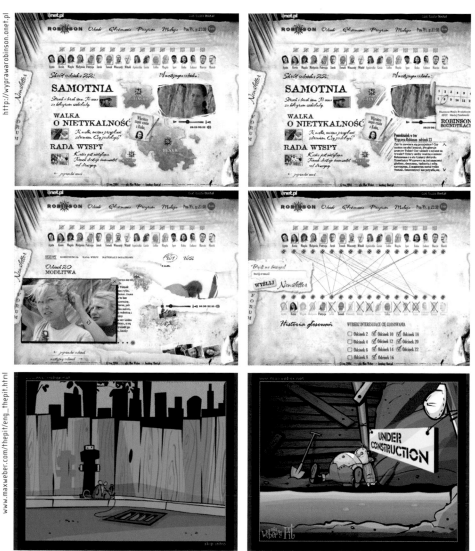

Location

ul. Saska 91

3 03-914 Warsaw

Poland

Contact

max@maxweber.com

Awards

Cannes Cyber Lion (Gold), Drum Portoroz (Silver), New York Festivals (Bronze), Golden Eagles, Flash Film Festival NY (Winner), Online Flash Film Festival (Winner), International Emmas (Winner), Reanimate (Winner), Netdiver Design Forte, Ultrashock BOMB SHOCK, Site of the Month Favourite Website Awards, etc.

Clients

Philips, Warner Bros, PDK, Eli Lilly, Sanitec, TVN, TVN7, ITI Group, etc.

MECANO

‹CANADA›

www.mecano.ca

Concept Functional and kinky. //// Fonctionnel et non conventionnel. //// Funktional und verrückt.

www.stefetmarie.com

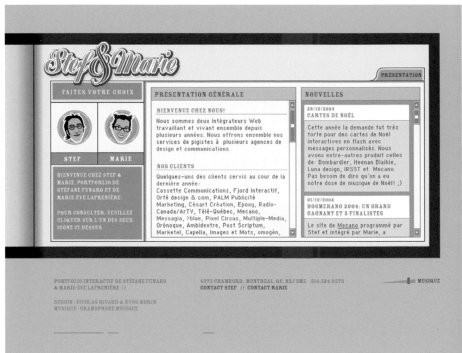

Name Mecano

Founded 2003

Team 1 Creative Director, 1 Art Director, 1 Flash Animator and Illustrator, 1 Flash Developer, 1 Web Developer, 1 Project Manager

Tools Macromedia Flash, AMFPHP, Flash Communication Server, etc.

Location

2056 St-Hubert
Montreal, Québec, H2L 3Z5
Canada

Contact

letsrock@mecano.ca

Awards

May 1st Reboot (Winner), Tiny Web Site Awards: Site of the Week,
Flash Favorite Web Site Awards: Site of the Day, Fcuk Star Award,
Boomerang Prices (Montréal), etc.

Clients

Mainly ad agencies and production companies (commercials, TV and
films).

MIRCO STUDIO

<ITALY/USA>

www.mircostudio.com

Concept

Our inspiration to create comes from our love for elegant technical solutions beautifully rendered. For this we pay homage to our homeland and its style that comes from the Italian soul. Form and function for us are one in the same - elegant, global, a feast for the senses as well as the intellect and the business world we compete in. We see every assignment - from the newest rich media PDA's to traditional print media - in the same way, as a challenge to create the extraordinary. //// Notre inspiration vient de notre penchant pour des solutions techniques élégantes superbement rendues. Nous rendons ici hommage à notre patrie et à son style, emprunt de l'âme italienne. La forme et la fonction sont pour nous une seule et même chose : élégante, globale, une fête pour les sens ainsi que pour l'intelligence et le monde des affaires dans lequel nous nous battons. Nous considérons chaque commande - du dernier ordinateur de poche aux médias d'impression traditionnels - de la même façon, comme un défi pour créer l'extraordinaire. //// Unsere Inspiration zur Kreation kommt aus der Liebe zu eleganten technischen Lösungen, wunderschön ausgeführt. Dies verdanken wir unserem Heimatland Italien und dem unvergleichlichen Stil, der uns im Blut liegt. Form und Funktion sind für uns eins - elegant, global, ein Fest für die Sinne, genauso wie die Intelligenzia und Geschäftswelt, in der wir uns behaupten müssen. Wir behandeln jeden Auftrag als Herausforderung, etwas ganz Aussergewöhnliches zu kreieren. Unabhängig davon, ob er von der neuesten, reichsten Medienagentur oder von den traditionellen Druckmedien kommt.

www.sillery.com

Name Mirco Studio

Founded 2002

Team 1 Art Director, 2 Code Developer, 1 Graphic Designer, 1 Web Designer, and 1 Copywriter.

Tools Html, Macromedia Flash, XML, PHP, Asp, etc.

www.frbh.com

www.skyworkscapital.com

Location

Piazza Garibaldi, 25

45100 Rovigo RO - ITALY

2 Stamford Landing, 68 Southfield Ave.

Stamford , CT 06902 - USA

Awards

IAC Internet Advertising Competition, LIAA, Cannes Lion (Silver),
Bardi Awards, Mediastar, Communication Arts Interactive Award,
Site of the Week Communication Arts, Macromedia Site of the Day
USA, etc.

Contact

info@mircostudio.com

Clients

Kings Super Markets, SkyWorks Capital, Connect US, De' Longhi Spa,
Boomerang Management, Zedlive.com, Gruppo Cardine San Paolo IMI,
Inc., Gruppo Gorla Spa, Efi Machine TotalGym, Provincia di Rovigo,
Francis-R Beverly Hills, Sebastian International, Depur Padana
Acque Spa, Sempre Rosso Blu, Fioritalia, Replay Blue Jeans, etc.

MOVE DESIGN

<USA>

www.movedesign.com

Using an integrated, problem-solving approach that addresses visual, structural and technical issues, Move Design creates relevant and engaging solutions to suit the individuality of their clients. Our work reflects a broad range of capabilities and interests, from corporate identity, graphic design and marketing collateral to web design, information architecture, user interface design, interactive prototypes and software development. //// Employant une méthode intégrée de résolution de problèmes visuels, structurels et techniques, Move Design crée des solutions appropriées et intéressantes adaptées à l'individualité de ses clients. Notre travail reflète un large éventail de compétences et d'intérêts aussi variés que l'image d'entreprise, le design graphique, le marketing collatéral, le design Web, l'architecture d'information, le design d'interfaces utilisateur, les prototypes interactifs ou encore le développement logiciel. //// Bei der Anwendung einer integrierten Problemstellung, die sich an visuelle, strukturelle sowie technische Aufgaben annähert, bietet MoveDesign relevante und brauchbare Lösungen, die die Individualität eines jeden Kunden garantiert. Unsere Arbeit reflektiert eine Vielzahl an Möglichkeiten und Interessen, angefangen von korporativer Identität über Grafikdesign und Marketing kollateral zu Webdesign, Informationsarchitektur, Nutzerdesign für Interface, interaktive Prototypen sowie Softwareentwicklung.

Adventure Zone Network – Adventure Travel Portal

Name: Move Design

Founded: 1998

Team: 2 Art Directors, and Contrators as needed.

Tools: Html, dhtml, XML, Javascript, Macromedia Flash, Macromedia Director, Macromedia Shockwave, etc.

ID Magazine

www.bridgedesign.com

Xuny - Online Urban Wear retailer

Location
1831 Powell Street
San Francisco, CA 94133
USA

Contact
info@movedesign.com

Awards
Communication Arts Magazine (various), Macromedia Site of the Day (various), I.D. Magazine, etc.

Clients
Apple, Compaq, Hewlett Packard, I.D. Magazine, Intel/Artmuseum. net, Intuit, Kodak, Logitech, Macromedia, Metronòm Gallery, Nike, One and Company, PeoplePC, Philips, Protozoa, Publicis & Hal Riney Advertising, Rioport, San Francisco MOMA, Sony, Stanford Learning Lab, Steelcase, Venture Collective, Xuny.com, etc.

PHORMA STUDIO

<ITALY>

www.phormastudio.com

Concept Our task is to give our clients the best in terms of quality, professionalism and contents care. //// Notre mission est de donner le meilleur à nos clients en termes de qualité, de professionnalisme et de contenu. //// Unser Ziel ist es, unseren Kunden das Beste in Qualität, Professionalität sowie bei der inhaltlichen Gestaltung zu bieten.

www.naive.it

Name Phorma Studio Design

Founded 2002

Team 2 Art Directors, and 1 Programmer.

Tools Macromedia Flash, html, Adobe Photoshop, Adobe Illustrator, PHP, etc.

Awards **Location**

Via del Tritone 87
Rome 00187
Italy

5.Francisco Flash Film Festival, Italian Art Directors Club Award,
Italian Web Awards, Favourite Web Award, etc.

Clients **Contact**

info@phormastudio.com

AC Milan, Sony, Telecom, Virgilio.it , Egotel, Hinnova Finance,
Fastweb, BPM, Casiraghi&Greco Advertisiment, Ufficiostile
Franchising, etc.

PIVOT

‹CANADA›

www.pivotdesign.ca

Concept

To apply the power of design to the task of business interactive communications. To make small voices mighty. To make things that are sensible into things that also move people. To open closed minds so that a message is understood, believed and welcomed. Pivot, Move the World. //// Pour appliquer le pouvoir du design aux communications interactives commerciales. Pour que tout le monde ait voix au chapitre. Pour rendre le raisonnable émouvant. Pour ouvrir les esprits fermés afin qu'un message puisse être compris, assimilé et bienvenu. Pivot fait bouger le monde. //// Die kraftvolle Energie des Designs für interaktive Geschäftskommunikation einsetzen. Zarte Stimmen mächtig erscheinen lassen. Sensibilität dafür nutzen, Massen zu bewegen. Engstirnige Menschen dazu zu bringen, eine Nachricht zu verstehen und sie ausserdem zu glauben und zu akzeptieren. Pivot, bewege die Welt.

www.yourhealthyhome.ca

THE ✚ LUNG ASSOCIATION™
YourHealthyHome

The Lung Association   Your Healthy Home   Partners   FAQ

Trees

Name   Pivot Design Communications Inc.

Founded   1998

Team   1 Creative Director, 1 Interactive Media Director, 2 Flash Designers, and 2 Programmers.

Tools   Macromedia Studio MX, and Adobe Creative Suite.

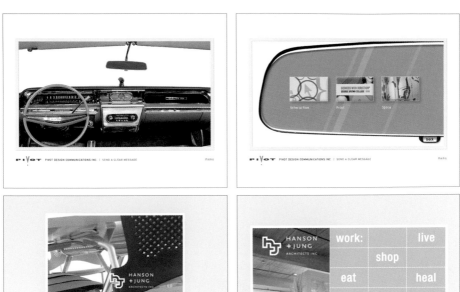

Location

65 George Street
Toronto, Ontario, M5A 4L8
Canada

Contact

design@pivotdesign.ca

Awards

The Advertising & Design Club of Canada, Applied Arts (various),
FWA, etc.

Clients

Amnesty International, CIHR - Canadian Institute of Health
Research, Ferrero Canada/Kinder Surprise, Heart & Stroke
Foundation, Labatt Breweries of Canada, LG Electronics, Lung
Association of Canada, Toronto Arts Council, Unitron Hearing, etc.

POSTVISUAL

<KOREA>

www.postvisual.com

Our work is aimed at changing web constantly into more interactive and organic media where people can share and expand their experiences. //// Notre travail vise à faire évoluer en permanence le Web en un média plus interactif et plus naturel où les gens peuvent partager et enrichir leurs expériences. //// Wir sind darauf bedacht, das Web ständig zu verändern, um es stets organischer und interaktiver werden zu lassen, ein Web, wo Menschen ihre Erfahrungen austauschen und erweitern können.

http://socool.curitel.com

CURITEL	So Cool is	**NEW** So Cool! ✹ Byul	So Cool! T-310V	So Cool! S4	So Cool! Jihoon	Make Your Cool

Name Postvisual

Founded 2000

Team 1 Art/Creative Director, 1 Producer, 3 Planners, 6 Designers, 3 Programmers, and 1 Action Scripter.

Tools Macromedia Flash, Adobe Photoshop, Adobe After Effects, etc.

misssixty

the Uninvited

Location

3rd Fl, 407-6 Seogyo-dong, Mapo-gu
Seoul, 121-840
Korea

Contact

postvisual@postvisual.com

Awards

Cannes Cyber Lion (Gold), New York Festivals Design Awards (Gold World Medal), Communication Arts Interactive, Flash Film Festival S.F., London International Awards Advertising & Design, Sundance Film Festival, Flash Film Festival NY, etc.

Clients

Nike, Pantech&Curitel, Samsung, Hyundai, LG Siltron, Hyosung, CJ Entertainment, Korea Entertainment, LJ Film, Sidus Film, Shincine Film, Bom Film, Taijin Media, Levi's, Avista(BNX), CDUX (Doll House), Shinsung Tongsang (Bros), Real Leaders (ASK), Samdo (Misssixty), ION, Joongang Media, Youngjin.com, Hyejiwon, etc.

PRELOADED

<UK>

www.preloaded.com

Concept

We're always trying to do that little bit more in everything we do. Attention to detail, depth and repeat visit value are things we build into all our projects. Our work is a labour of love. It's considered and planned on many levels, especially how different people will find their own ways of interacting with something that engages them. Hence our motto… preloaded, we do nice things… //// Nous essayons toujours d'apporter un petit plus à tout ce que nous faisons. Le souci du détail, la profondeur et l'importance donnée aux visites répétées sont intégrés à tous nos projets. Nos solutions sont le fruit d'un travail réalisé avec amour. Elles sont réfléchies et planifiées à de nombreux niveaux, et résolvent en particulier le problème de savoir comment des personnes différentes peuvent trouver la manière de communiquer avec quelque chose qui les séduit. D'où notre devise… Nous faisons de belles choses… //// Wir versuchen stets, etwas mehr zu geben, als von uns verlangt wird. Detailtreue, Profundität sowie ständige Betreuung ist in unseren Projekten verankert. Unsere Arbeit ist eine Arbeit voller Liebe. Sie ist auf verschiedenen Ebenen durchstrukturiert, besonders im Hinblick auf die Schwierigkeiten, die so viele haben, in der interaktiven Welt ihren ganz persönlichen Weg zu finden. Folglich lautet unser Motto… preloaded, wir machen gute Sachen…

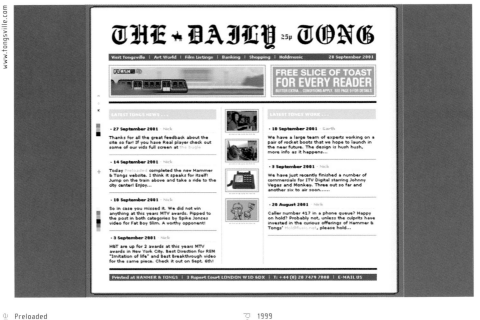

Name
Preloaded

Founded
1999

Team
2 Developer, 1 New Business Director, 1 Creative Director,
1 Office Manager, 1 Designer, 1 Production Director,
1 Art Director, and 1 Information Architecture.

Tools
Macromedia Flash, Adobe Photoshop, Discreet 3D Studio Max,
Adobe After Effects, Macromedia Dreamweaver, Macromedia
Fireworks, etc.

Location

16-24 Underwood Street
N1 7JQ London
United Kingdom

Contact

studio@preloaded.com

Awards

5X5W, BAFTA, BIMA, FlashintheCan, IVCA, Flash Forward,
Macromedia Showcase site, NMA Effectiveness,
Ultrashock Shocked Site, etc.

Clients

MTV, BBC, Coca-Cola, Sony, EMI, Universal, Hammer & Tongs, Mother,
Microsoft, Nike, etc.

PQC STUDIO

<TAIWAN>

www.pqcstudio.com.tw

Concept

We bring marketing strategy, creativeness and technology together to ensure our client's web site represents the foremost essence of their company, their products, their vision, and their service. //// Nous conjuguons stratégie marketing, créativité et technologie pour garantir que le site Web de notre client reflète l'essence suprême de son entreprise, ses produits, sa philosophie et ses services. //// Wir verbinden Marketingstrategien, Kreativität und Technologie um sicher zu gehen, dass die Webseite unseres Kunden das Wesentliche seiner Firma, seiner Produkte und Vision sowie seines Service repräsentiert.

www.pqcstudio.com.tw

Name PQC Studio

Founded 1994

Team 1 Creative Director, 2 Programmers, 3 Graphic Designers, 2 Flash Designers, 1 Marketing Representative, and 1 System Engineer.

Tools Html, Macromedia Flash, dhtml, PHP, Asp, JavaScript, CSS, Adobe After Effects, etc.

Location

Hsing Yi Road Lane 89,
Number 1 Taipei
Taiwan ROC

Contact

pqcstudio@pqcstudio.com.tw

Awards

None

Clients

American Chamber of Commerce (Taipei), Audi (Taiwan branch), BAS
PENS, Canadian Trade Office (Taipei), Community Services Center,
Institut Francais (Taipei), Interserv, Italian economic, Trade And
Cultural Promotion Office, Parsons Brinckerhoff, Siemens, Protel
Pacific Corporation, etc.

PROJECTOR

<SWEDEN>

www.projector.se

Concept — Leveraging the potential of the interactive communication with a combination of creativity and modern technology. //// Multiplier le potentiel de la communication interactive en conjuguant créativité et technologie moderne. //// Wir bedienen uns des Potentials der interaktiven Kommunikation und kombinieren es mit kreativer und moderner Technologie.

www.gb.se

Name — Projector

Founded — 1993

Team — 1 Creative Director, 3 Art Directors, 1 Copywriter, 2 Flash Developers, 2 Web Designers, 1 Developer, and 2 Project Managers.

Tools — Macromedia Flash, html, etc.

Location

Grev Magnigatan 4
114 55 Stockholm
Sweden

Contact

info@projector.se

Awards

FWA (Winner), Cannes Lion (Final), LIAA: Final (various),
Macromedia Flash: Site of the Day, Cresta Awards (Winner),
Brons New York Festival, etc.

Clients

Absolut Vodka, Bonnier, Bostream, Clear Channel, Electrolux,
EMI Music, Emma Förlag, First Hotels, Flynordic, Hasseludden,
Spendrups, Svenskt Näringsliv, SVT, TCO, Unilever Bestfoods
(GB Glace), etc.

PURE COMMUNICATION

\<BELGIUM\>

www.pure-communication.be

Concept

Rather than to think of the Internet as a place that merely needs web development, we consider the web a medium to showcase ideas, creativity and above all: design in its purest form. Hence the company name, Pure Communication. Anything that leaves our desktops is guaranteed to be pure, simple, efficient and well designed. //// Plutôt que penser l'Internet comme un lieu où seul le développement Web est nécessaire, nous le considérons comme un moyen d'offrir une vitrine à des idées, à la créativité et surtout : au design sous sa forme la plus pure. D'où le nom de notre entreprise, Pure Communication. Tout ce qui est passé par nos bureaux est garanti pur, simple, efficace et bien conçu. //// Anstatt das Internet als etwas zu betrachten, das hauptsächlich Webentwicklung braucht, sehen wir es eher als ein Medium, unsere Ideen, Kreativität und vor allem Design in seiner reinsten Form darzustellen. Daher der Name, Pure communication. Ganz gleich was unseren Schreibtisch verlässt, es ist garantiert rein, einfach, leistungsfähig und mit einem guten Design.

www.vanhavermaet.be

Name PURE COMMUNICATION

Founded 2000

Team 2 Creative Partners/Designers, 1 Developer, and a bunch of freelance Designers, Programmers, Copywriters, Photographers, etc.

Tools Macromedia Flash, html, XML, Macromedia Fireworks, Adobe Photoshop, etc.

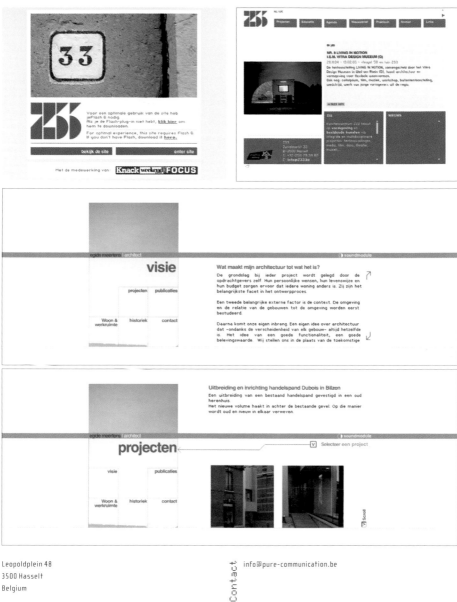

Location | Leopoldplein 48
3500 Hasselt
Belgium

Contact | info@pure-communication.be

Awards | None

Clients | Africa Museum, Architect Egide Meertens, Axa, Caw 'T Verschil,
Cleuren-Merken Architecten, Clockwise, Coca Cola, Groep T, Kamer
Van Koophandel, LG&f, Provincie Limburg, Proximus, Samsonite, SN
Brussels, Suzuki, Tele Atlas, Toyota, Van Havermaet, Vandeputte
Groep, VRT, etc.

R/GA

<USA>
www.rga.com

Concept To reach today's consumers in the online space, it takes more than stunning visuals to capture their attention. We believe one of the secrets to our success is creating sites with branded content that tell stories and engage users. //// Pour toucher les consommateurs d'aujourd'hui dans l'espace en ligne, il faut davantage qu'un visuel captivant. Selon nous, l'un des secrets de notre succès est que nous créons des sites à contenu de marque qui racontent des histoires et séduisent les internautes. //// Um heutzutage den Verbraucher online zu erreichen und seine Aufmerksamkeit zu erregen, bedarf es mehr als nur optischer Reize. Wir glauben, unser Geheimnis zum Erfolg liegt darin, dass wir Seiten für Markenprodukte kreieren, die Geschichten erzählen und somit den Verbraucher fesseln.

www.nikeid.com

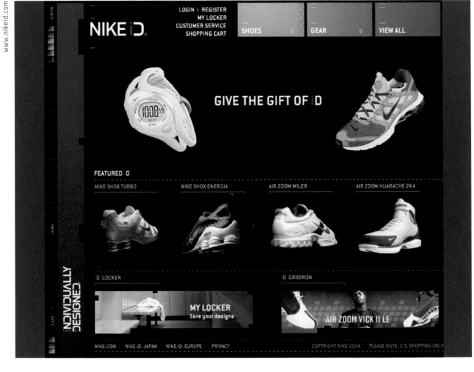

Name R/GA

Founded 1977

Team Collaborative team model that consists of Account Directors, Copywriters, Designers, Interaction Designers, Producers, Strategists, and Technology Leads.

Tools Diverse tools, including Macromedia Flash, XML, J2EE, .NET, depending on the scope and needs of the client project. Also favor solutions that are flexible and extendable, such as XML-driven Flash and CSS-linked semantic XHTML to separate presentation from content.

Location

350 West 39th Street
New York, NY 10018
USA

Contact

web@rga.com

Awards

In both 2003 and 2004 alone, R/GA won nearly 100 awards at some
of the industry's most prestigious competitions, including Cannes
Cyber Lions, Clios, London International Advertising Awards, and
One Show Interactive.

Clients

Avaya, Bank of America, Bed Bath & Beyond, Circuit City, IBM, Levi
Strauss, Purina, Nike, Reuters, Subaru, Target, Verizon, etc.

ROOTYLICIOUS

\<CROATIA\>

www.rootylicious.com

8
5

Concept

Simple and Rooty. //// *Simple et authentique.* //// **Einfach und mit Wurzel.**

www.rootylicious.com

Name Rootylicious.studios

Founded 2000

Team 2 Main Designers, 1 Programmer, and freelance Designers on project demand.

Tools Macromedia Studio MX, Adobe Creative Suite, and Text Edit.

148 · BEST STUDIOS

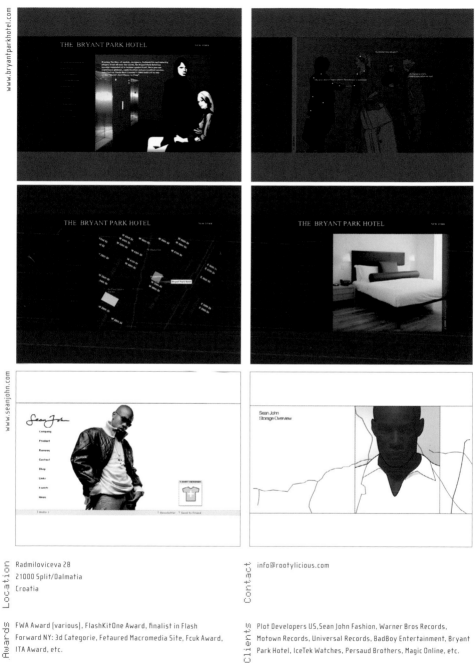

www.bryantparkhotel.com

THE BRYANT PARK HOTEL

www.seanjohn.com

Location

Radmiloviceva 28
21000 Split/Dalmatia
Croatia

Awards

FWA Award (various), FlashKitOne Award, finalist in Flash
Forward NY: 3d Categorie, Fetaured Macromedia Site, Fcuk Award,
ITA Award, etc.

Contact

info@rootylicious.com

Clients

Plot Developers US, Sean John Fashion, Warner Bros Records,
Motown Records, Universal Records, BadBoy Entertainment, Bryant
Park Hotel, IceTek Watches, Persaud Brothers, Magic Online, etc.

SCHOLZ & VOLKMER

<GERMANY>

www.s-v.de

Concept

For more than ten years Scholz & Volkmer crafts interactive applications that stand out through creative concepts, intuitive navigation and lean backend solutions. With strong enthusiasm for what's new, the courage to change and an eye for the essential, Scholz & Volkmer succeeds in making people curious again and again. Curious? //// Scholz & Volkmer crée depuis plus de dix ans des applications interactives qui se distinguent de par leurs concepts créatifs, leur navigation intuitive et leurs solutions backend épurées. Avec son enthousiasme pour la nouveauté, le courage d'évoluer et le sens de l'essentiel, Scholz & Volkmer parvient à rendre les gens curieux, encore et toujours. Cela éveille-t-il votre curiosité ? //// Seit zehn Jahren macht Scholz & Volkmer interaktive Anwendungen, die sich durch kreative Konzepte, intuitive Nutzerführung und schlanke Backendlösungen auszeichnen. Mit Begeisterung für Neues, Mut zur Veränderung und den Blick für das Wesentliche gelingt es dabei, Menschen immer wieder neugierig zu machen. Neugierig?

www.acht-frankfurt.de

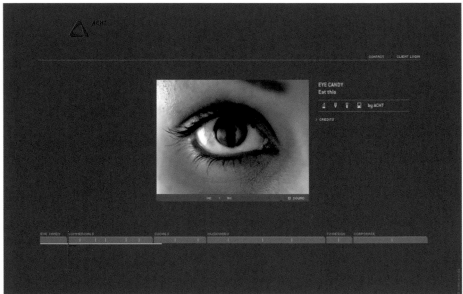

Name
Scholz & Volkmer

Founded
1994

Team
1 Managing Director, 1 Creative Director, 1 Technical Director and 45 professionals working on design, programming, project management, and administration.

Tools
Homesite, Macromedia Dreamweaver, Macromedia Flash, XML Spy, Eclipse, PHP Edit, UltraEdit, etc.

www.mercedes-benz.com/mixedtape

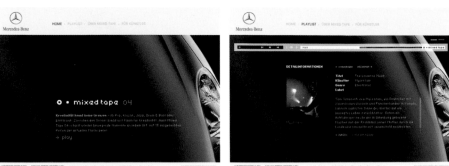

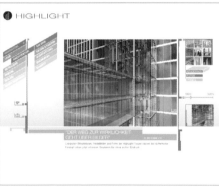

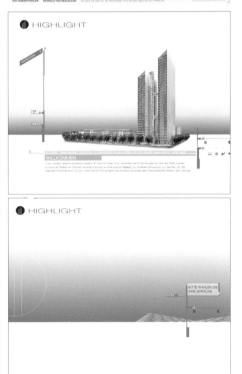

www.highlight-towers.com

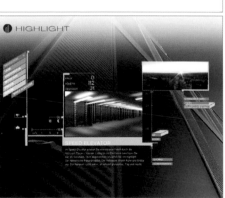

Location

Schwalbacher Str. 76
D - 65183 Wiesbaden
Germany

Awards

More than 100 national (in Germany) and 220 international design
prizes. Among them Grand Prix at the Cyber Lions and 6 Cyber Lions
in Cannes, 6 Awards at the ADC NY, 3 Clio Awards and 9 Nails at the
ADC Germany.

Contact

mail@s-v.de

Clients

DaimlerChrysler, E.ON, Fraport, Ingo Maurer, Mercedes-Benz,
O2 Germany, Toni Gard, Rui Camilo, USM, Vogue, etc.

SENTIDOWEB

<ARGENTINA>

www.sentidoweb.com.ar

Sentidoweb : design in motion. //// Sentidoweb : le design en mouvement. //// Sentidoweb: Design in Bewegung.

www.ipworldcomm.com.ar

Name   Sentidoweb

Founded   2001

Team   1 Art Director, 1 Programmer, 2 Designers, and 1 Commercial.

Tools   Macromedia Flash, Discreet 3D Studio Max, html, Asp, etc.

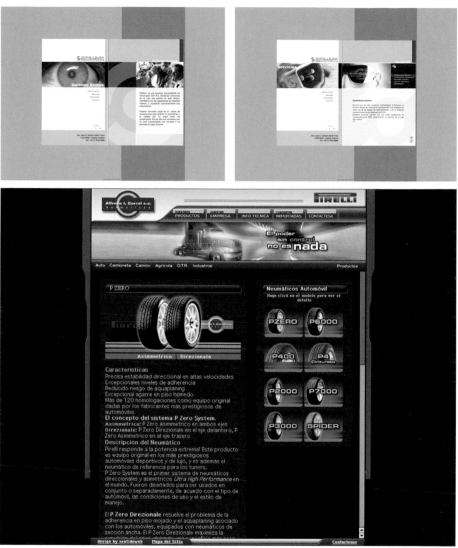

Awards Location

Yatay 386
1184 Buenos Aires
Argentina

WebPick, RGB, and ABWE.

Contact

info@sentidoweb.com.ar

Clients

BDO Consulting, Xioma Consultores, Neumáticos Alfredo L. Corral
S.A., Yellowstone travel, Sirilium IT Consulting, DCL Consultores,
IPworldcomm, etc.

SPILL.NET

<FRANCE>

www.spill.net

Concept

A constant, unceasing desire to be innovators... //// L'envie sans cesse renouvelée d'être innovant... //// Ein ständiges, nicht aufhörendes Verlangen, innovativ zu sein...

www.colette.fr

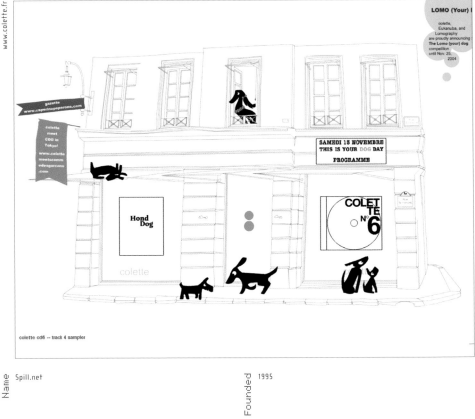

Name: Spill.net

Founded: 1995

Team: 2 Creative/Art Directors, 2 Programmers, 2 Project Managers, 3 Designers, and several Interns.

Tools: Paper, Pencils, Macromedia Flash, XML, PHP, MySQL, etc.

www.lescheminsblancs.fr

www.ikepod.com

Location Paris
France

Awards Webby Award, ID interactive award, etc.

Contact contact@spill.net

Clients Fondation Cartier pour l'art contemporain, colette, Marie-Hélène de Taillac, Marc Newson, AOL/Time Warner, CondeNet, etc.

STONEWALL

<SOUTH AFRICA>

www.stonewallproductions.com

Concept

Stonewall Productions is a next generation online marketing agency that creates innovative client-driven digital and online solutions that deliver measurable results. //// Stonewall Productions est une agence de marketing en ligne de nouvelle génération qui crée des solutions en ligne numériques innovantes à l'écoute des clients et donnant des résultats quantifiables. //// Stonewall Productions ist eine zukunftsorientierte online-Marketingagentur, die innovative und kundenbezogene Problemlösungen digital sowie online bietet.

www.5fm.co.za

Name Stonewall Productions

Founded 1997

Team 1 Creative Director, 2 Senior Designers, 1 Junior Designer,
1 Flash Developer, 2 Programmers, 1 Project Manager,
1 Business Director, and 1 Managing Director.

Tools Macromedia Flash, xhtml, CSS, XML, Asp, PHP, Java, etc.

www.millertime.co.za

www.carolinevos.com

Location

201 Regent Place, 30 Regent Road,
Sea Point, Cape Town
South Africa

Awards

Construction New Media Awards (Gold).

Contact

info@stonewallproductions.com

Clients

Microsoft, Volkswagen, SAB Miller, First National Bank, SITA,
Virgin Active, 5fm, SABC Radio, Jack Daniels, Redbull, Old Mutual,
Lowe Bull, FNB, etc.

TAK!TAK!

<UK>

www.taktak.net

Concept: Bold. Simple. Confident. //// Audacieux. Simple. Assuré. //// Frech. Einfach. Vertraulich.

www.mediumrarestore.com

Name: tak!TAK!

Founded: As an entity: 1995
As a design studio: 2004

Team: 1 Creative Director/Designer, 1 Technical Director, and a small network of freelance Artists, Designers and Programmers.

Tools: Pen. Paper. Mac. Mouse. Screen. Html. Macromedia Flash. Asp. XML. (In that order)

Location

115 Custard Factory, Gibb Street
B9 4AA Birmingham
UK

Contact

contact@taktak.net

Awards

Best Art Website SXSW Awards (StickerNation.Net).

Clients

Medium Rare, StickerNation.Net, Pinpops, Blowback, YKiki, etc.

TOCQUIGNY
‹USA›
www.tocquigny.com

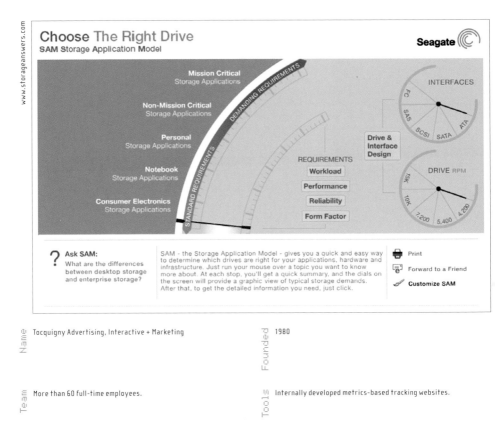

TOCQUIGNY
ADVERTISING | INTERACTIVE | MARKETING

Concept

Our web technologies such as response tracking and behavioral targeting will allow companies to move their electronic marketing and web sites from static content to a medium by which they can serve relevant offers and content, while generating incremental additional revenue and drive increased ROI. //// Nos technologies Web, le "response tracking" et le "behavioral targeting" en particulier, permettent aux entreprises de faire de leur marketing électronique et de leurs sites Web, caractérisés par un contenu statique, un moyen par lequel elles peuvent proposer des offres et du contenu pertinent, tout en générant un revenu supplémentaire incrémentiel et un retour sur investissements accru. //// Unsere Webtechnologien - z.B. bei der Verfolgung von Rückmeldungen und Verhaltensweisen - ermöglichen es Firmen, ihr elektronisches Marketing und ihre statischen Webseiten in ein neues Medium zu verwandeln, bei dem sie sich wichtige Angebote sowie Information zunutze machen können und ausserdem zusätzliche Einkommen sowie einen steigenden Ertrag des investierten Kapitals vermerken können.

www.storageanswers.com

Name Tocquigny Advertising, Interactive + Marketing

Founded 1980

Team More than 60 full-time employees.

Tools Internally developed metrics-based tracking websites.

Location

901 S. Mopac, Building 1, Suite 100

Austin, TX 78746

USA

Contact

ideas@tocquigny.com

Awards

Tocquigny has received 100's of honors and awards for creativity such as One Show, local, regional and national Addys, New York Art Director's Club, and Communication Arts. The Austin Business Journal ranked Tocquigny the # 1 Web Development Team.

Clients

Dell Inc., Seagate Technologies, Caterpillar, etc.

TONIC

‹UK›

www.tonic.co.uk

Tonic aim to bring a fresh perspective to online design - combining strong creative concepts, traditional design values and the latest interactive technologies. //// *Tonic a vocation a apporter une nouvelle perspective au design en ligne, en conjuguant des concepts créatifs forts, des valeurs de design traditionnelles et des technologies interactives de pointe.* //// **Tonic möchte eine frische Perspektive in das Online- Design bringen, indem wir starke, kreative Konzepte mit traditionellem Design und den neuesten interaktiven Technologien verbinden.**

www.750mph.com

tonic

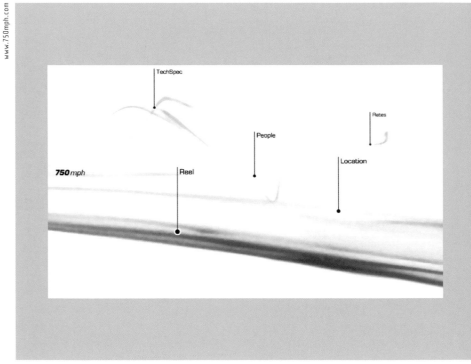

Name	Tonic	Founded	1998

| Team | 1 Creative Director, 2 Design Directors, 6 Designers, 4 Flash Designers, and 1 Programmer. Total staff number is 25 plus. | Tools | Macromedia Flash, XML, Java, PHP, html, dhtml, etc. |

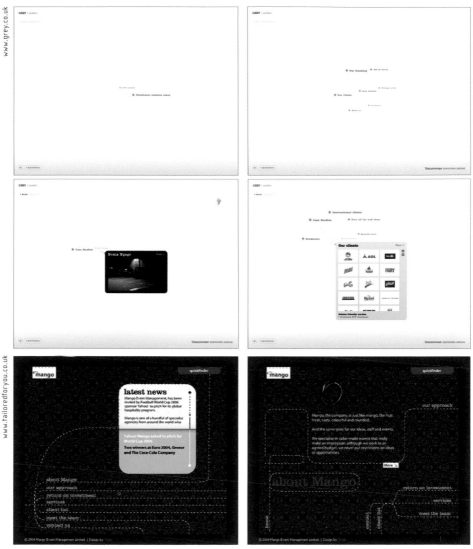

Location

141-143 Shoreditch High Street
E1 6JE London
United Kingdom

Contact

design@tonic.co.uk

Awards

Design Council Innovation Award, International Society of
Typographic Designers Excellence Award, Dutch TMF Award, New
Media Age Effectiveness Award, Auto Express, Interactive Music
Nomination, BIMA Website Nomination, D&AD Silver Nomination,
Design Week Website Nomination, etc.

Clients

Sony Europe, Vodafone, MTV Networks Europe, Victor Chandler,
D&AD, V&A Museum, Polydor, etc.

TRANSPORTER

‹AUSTRIA›

www.transporter.at

Concept We deliver an individual and tailored solution for each client and seek to provide a web-experience that triggers curiosity and delight. //// Nous fournissons à chaque client une solution individuelle taillée sur mesure et cherchons à assurer une expérience Web suscitant la curiosité et le plaisir. //// Wir liefern massgeschneiderte Lösungen für jeden Kunden und sind ständig darauf bedacht, mit unseren Webseiten Neugierde und Entzücken hervorzurufen.

www.transporter.at

Name Transporter* visual design and communication

Founded 2000

Team 3 Directors, and a team of Freelancers and Consultants to meet any challenge.

Tools Add Macromedia Flash, PHP, MySQL, html to analytic talks, open eyes, open minds, and lots of time.

Location

Innstrasse 77

A-6020 Innsbruck

Austria

Contact

lounge@transporter.at

Awards

Favourite Website Award, Design Forte Award, etc.

Clients

Transporter attracts many clients within the fields of art, architecture and design looking for specific, individual, and unique solutions.

VARIOUSWAYS

<USA>

www.variousways.com

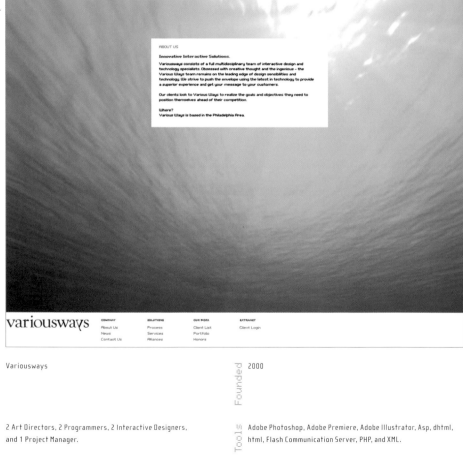

variousways

variousways

Concept

Variousways is obsessed with creative thought, always pushing the limits of cutting edge interactive design. //// Variousways a pour obsession la pensée créatrice et repousse sans cesse les limites du design interactif d'avant-garde. //// Kreatives Denken ist unsere Obsession, immer den Anschlag zum Limit suchend, bei einschlagendem Design.

www.variousways.com

Name Variousways

Founded 2000

Team 2 Art Directors, 2 Programmers, 2 Interactive Designers, and 1 Project Manager.

Tools Adobe Photoshop, Adobe Premiere, Adobe Illustrator, Asp, dhtml, html, Flash Communication Server, PHP, and XML.

www.bornmagazine.org/projects/nevergrow

www.gecko9.com

Location

7936 Montgomery Ave, Elkins Park,
PA 19027
USA

Contact

info@variousways.com

Awards

Philly Gold Awards, American Design Awards, Graphis
Interactive Design Annual, Netdiver Design Forte Award, Create
Online Magazine. Recognition: thebestdesigns.com, coolhomepages.
com, Intervibes Recognition Award, Media Inspiration Award,
www.K10K.com, www.newstoday.com, etc.

Clients

American Express, Arts Sojourn, Barrett N Smith, Bella Bocce, Born
Magazine, Charter Partners, Checkpoint Systems, Covanta Energy,
Digitalwave, Erims, Healthtrac, J.T.Baker, Keefe, Bruyette & Woods,
Jonjon, K'nex, Lancaster General, Martin Memorial, Medimmune,
Orasure, Patt White, Perkin Elmer, Prolog Internet Service, etc.

VELOCITY STUDIO

<CANADA>
www.velocitystudio.com

Concept

Velocity is a creative house that is very relaxed in terms of rules. We are a small group of tight knit friends who all want to succeed for the greater good of the company. We see ourselves as team players that know how a business should be run and know how our clients and partners should be treated. We believe in the "old school" business tactics of putting our best creative foot forward and to always under promise and over deliver. //// Velocity est un groupe de création très cool en matières de règles. Nous formons un groupe d'amis proches qui souhaitent tous réussir dans l'intérêt de leur entreprise. Nous nous considérons comme des équipiers qui savent comment mener une entreprise et comment leurs clients et partenaires doivent être traités. Nous croyons en la tactique commerciale "old school" consistant à privilégier la création, à ne rien promettre et à donner beaucoup. //// Velocity ist ein kreatives Haus und sehr relaxed, wenn es um Regeln geht. Wir sind eine Gruppe enger Freunde und alle darauf bedacht, Erfolg für unsere gemeinsame Firma zu erzielen. Wir sehen uns als Teamplayer, die alle wissen, wie ein Geschäft funktioniert und wie wir unsere Kunden und Partner zu behandeln haben. Wir glauben an die "alte Schule" und ihre Geschäftsphilosophie, die darauf beläuft, unseren bestmöglichen kreativen Schritt zu tun und stets weniger zu versprechen als wir später liefern.

velocitystudio.com

Name Velocity Studio & Associates

Founded 2001

Team 3 Creative Directors, 2 Flash Designers, and 2 Programmers.

Tools Cinema 4D, Adobe Photoshop, Macromedia Flash, XML, etc.

434 Maitland St. Suite #1
London, ON
N6B 2Z2, Canada

info@velocitystudio.com

Velocity has been awarded in many ocasions for its creative
achievements.

American Online, Team One Advertising, Saatchi & Saatchi, The
Hearst Corporation, WIRED Magazine, Labbats, Rothmans Benson &
Hedges, Six Flags Theme Park, Shure Technologies, Matthew Good,
GoodLife Fitness Canada, etc.

VIRTUALNET

‹BRAZIL›

www.virtualnet.com.br

Concept

Extreme design that takes advantage of Internet interaction seducing the user and accomplishing any campaigns' goals. //// Des design extrêmes tirant parti de l'interaction d'Internet, séduisant ainsi l'utilisateur et atteignant les objectifs de n'importe quelle campagne publicitaire. //// Extremes Design, das sich die Interaktion im Netz zu nutzen macht, indem der Verbraucher verführt und somit das Ziel jeglicher Kampagne erreicht wird.

identidade

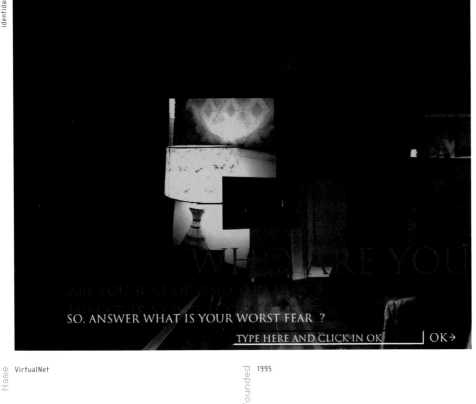

SO, ANSWER WHAT IS YOUR WORST FEAR ?

TYPE HERE AND CLICK IN OK | OK→

Name VirtualNet

Founded 1995

Team 1 Creative/Art Director/Motion Designer, 1 Flash Programer, 2 Programers, and 2 Motion Designers.

Tools Motion Design, Macromedia Flash, Adobe After Effects, dhtml, Dotnet, etc.

Location

263, Funchal Street
São Paulo
Brazil

Contact

bonfim@virtualnet.com.br

Awards

Cannes Lions, Bienal of Graffic Design, etc.

Clients

Columbia Pictures, Buena Vista internationa,
Walt Disney Pictures, etc.

VIS-TEK

<SPAIN>

www.vis-tek.net

Concept
One half of visual work + One half of technic work = VIS-TEK, this is the perfect recipe! //// 50% de travail visuel + 50% de travail technique = VIS-TEK, la formule idéale ! //// 50% visuelle Arbeit + 50% technische Arbeit = VIS-TEK, das perfekte Rezept!

www.lunxialtre.com

Name VIS-TEK Barcelona

Founded 2002

Team 2 Art Directors, 1 Graphic Designer, 1 Graphic Assistant, 1 Flash Designer, and 1 Programmer.

Tools Macromedia Flash, Adobe Premiere, Adobe After Effects, pencil and paper.

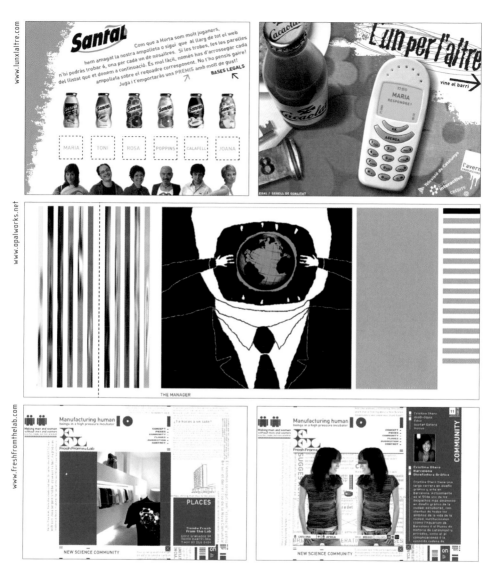

www.lunxlaftre.com

www.opalworks.net

www.freshfromthelab.com

Location

Av. Marquès d'Argentera 17, Pral 2.

08003 - Bacelona

Spain

Contact

hola@vis-tek.net

Awards

DRAC Awards (various), ADCE, LAUS Awards, COMPUTER SPACE, etc.

Clients

Internom-Oxfam, Universitat Oberta de Catalunya (UOC), Pepe Jeans London, Fresh from the Lab, Opalworks, Adg-Fad, CCRTVI (TV3), Reed Exhibitions, Hotusa, Sercotel, Booket - Ed. Planeta, Thyssen-Bornemiza Museum, etc.

WEB WORKSTYLE

<GERMANY>

www.web-workstyle.com

Concept
I love my work and I think that who does not love his/hers should not torment others with it. //// J'aime mon travail et estime que quiconque ne peut pas en dire autant devrait se se faire tout petit. //// Ich liebe meine Arbeit und ich bin der Meinung, wer seine Arbeit nicht liebt, sollte andere damit nicht quälen.

www.rondoveneziano.com

Name Web Workstyle®

Founded 2002

Team 1 Managing/Art Director/Programmer/Flash Designer,
1 Art Director/Flash Designer/Translator/Corrector,
1 Translator/Corrector, and 1 Branch Manager.

Tools Homesite, Macromedia Flash, Discreet 3D Studio Max, etc.

www.starcknetwork.com

www.screen-shots.com

www.marcushansen.com

Location

Hugo-Lang-Bogen 65
D-81735 Munich
Germany

Contact

info@web-workstyle.com

Awards

Golden Web Award (various), Meilleur site par bonweb (various),
Canadian Web, Art Space World Web Award (various), Webmaster
award, Gold Artsy Award, Golden Award excellence of design, etc.

Clients

Philippe Starck, Rondò Veneziano, Berengo Fine Arts Murano, Marcus
Hansen, Augustiner Bräu München, La Stanza, Orlando Restaurant,
First Hotel, etc.

WORLDOPTIMIZER

<GERMANY>

www.worldoptimizer.com

Concept — Information has to prickle and flow. //// L'information doit fuser et affluer. //// Information muss kitzeln und fliessen.

www.worldoptimizer.com

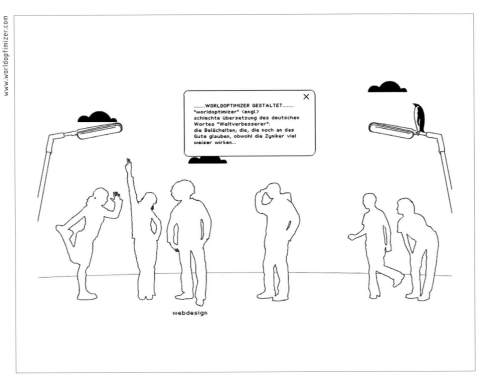

........WORLDOPTIMIZER GESTALTET........
"worldoptimizer" <engl.>
schlechte Übersetzung des deutschen
Wortes "Weltverbesserer":
die Belächelten; die, die noch an das
Gute glauben, obwohl die Zyniker viel
weiser wirken...

webdesign

Name — Worldoptimizer

Founded — 2001

Team — 1 Art Director, 3 Graphic Designers, 2 Programmers, 1 Photographer, 1 Product Designer, and 1 Concept Designer.

Tools — Macromedia Flash, BBEdit, and Macromedia Freehand and Adobe Photoshop are the choice for illustrations and data import.

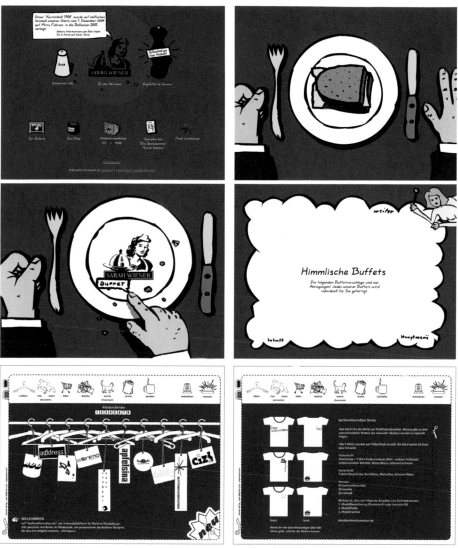

Awards   Location   Kastanienallee 40
10119 Berlin
Germany

Many site hits.

Contact   mail@worldoptimizer.com

Clients   maß.1, tv5, Live From Death Row, francophonic festival, creative
game verlag, Auswärtiges Amt Paris, Nachhaltiger Filmblick, DZZM
bat-Studiotheater, Vobis, Arbeit und Leben, etc.

WYSIWYG*
‹GERMANY›
www.wysiwyg.de

wysiwyg
software design

Concept A client once noted that wysiwyg* actually isn't a real multimedia agency. We actually liked the idea. wysiwyg* is rather an operating system that invents and makes useful and cool things using digital media. //// Un client nous a un jour fait la remarque que wysiwyg* n'est pas vraiment une agence multimédia. Nous avons aimé cette idée. wysiwyg* est en effet davantage un système d'exploitation qui invente et crée des choses utiles ou cool à l'aide de données numériques. //// Ein Kunde hat einmal gesagt, wir wären gar keine Multimedia-Agentur. Das fanden wir gut. Denn wysiwyg* ist ein Betriebssystem - zum Erfinden und Kreieren von Lösungen in elektronischen Medien.

www.wysiwyg.de/zufriedometer/zufriedometer.php

Name wysiwyg* software design GmbH

Founded 1994

Team 3 Project Managers, 7 Art Directors/Screen Designers, 6 Programmers, 1 Concept/Copy Writer, 1 CEO, 1 Technical Director, and 1 Creative Director. 20 Employees overall.

Tools Html, PHP, Macromedia Flash, dhtml, XML, java, Macromedia Director, etc.

Location

Stresemannstrasse 26
D-40210 Düsseldorf
Germany

Contact

info@wysiwyg.de

Awards

iF Design Award (various), red dot award, BOB Award Bronze, ADC,
Annual Multimedia, Deutscher Preis für Kommunikationsdesign,
Annual Multimedia, Deutscher Preis für Kommunikationsdesign,
Rheingold Award, etc.

Clients

Lufthansa, Deutsche Telekom, Deutsche Bank, TDK, start/Amadeus,
Toshiba, Volvic, Microsoft, SONY, RWE, Siemens, Wacom, vizzavi,
Persil, Krombacher, BEGA, vodafone, premiere world, we|come|24,
Rheinische Post Online, SPD, Cap Gemini, Total Recall, Pohlschröder,
Rempen & Partner, SEGA, Henkel, Spiegel Online, etc.

XNET

⟨SWEDEN⟩

www.xnet.se

TM

xnet.se

We are a web production company. //// Nous sommes une entreprise de production Web. //// Wir sind eine Web-Produktionsfirma.

MÄSSOR/UTSTÄLLNINGAR

SEB på Expo 2000 i Hannover

Uppdrag: Visa Europa att SEB, som just köpt tyska banken BFG, är en stark aktör. En visionär svensk bank i teknikens framkant. **Insikt:** SEB måste leva som de lär. Från klädsel till teknisk utrustning och inredning. **Så gjorde vi:** Utställning i två delar inrymd i svenska paviljongen. Specialdesignad och byggd från grunden. Ett Today Room där SEB:s senaste tjänster ochÉ

MER ▶

EVENTS

PORTFOLIO

KNOCK ACTION MARKETING   Kungsgatan 5 Box 7103 SE-103 87 Stockholm Sweden   Tel +46 8 21 74 84   Fax +46 8 21 68 10   info@knock.se

Name Xnet	**Founded** 1996
Team 3 Designers, 1 Programmer, and additional professionals in their network to respond on demand.	**Tools** Macromedia Flash, and various 3D and animation programs.

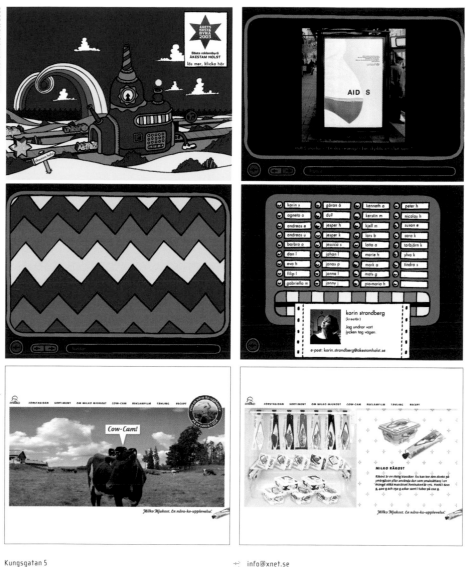

Location

Kungsgatan 5
10387 Stockholm
Sweden

Contact

info@xnet.se

Awards

Most recently awarded in Cannes Lions and Golden Egg Awards.

Clients

Posten (Swedish Postal Service), Absolut Vodka, Flicka,
Guldägget, etc.

YEEDA DESIGN
<INDIA>
www.yeedadesign.com

Concept

Affordable quality solutions delivered remotely. //// *Des solutions de qualité peu onéreuses fournies à distance.* //// Bezahlbare, qualitative Lösungen aus der Ferne geliefert.

www.indexventures.com

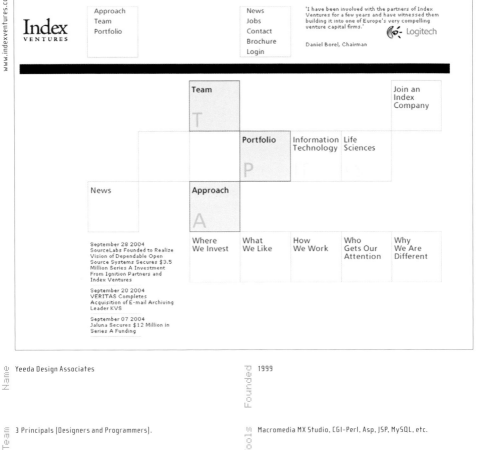

Name Yeeda Design Associates

Founded 1999

Team 3 Principals (Designers and Programmers).

Tools Macromedia MX Studio, CGI-Perl, Asp, JSP, MySQL, etc.

Location

38 Rest House Road,
Bangalore 560001
INDIA

Contact

info@yeedadesign.com

Awards

None

Clients

Index Ventures, Assn. des Anciens de L'Ecolint, European Foundation
for Entrepreneurship Research, Innovative Silicon, Kimotion
Technologies, SpinX Technologies, Walker's France, Senthil
Photography, Sebo, Bysoft, Aramis Auto, Elegant Choice, etc.

ZENTROPY

<GERMANY>
www.zentropypartners.de

Concept — Life Changing Experiences. //// Des expériences qui changent la vie. //// Eine lebensverändernde Erfahrung.

www.condor.de

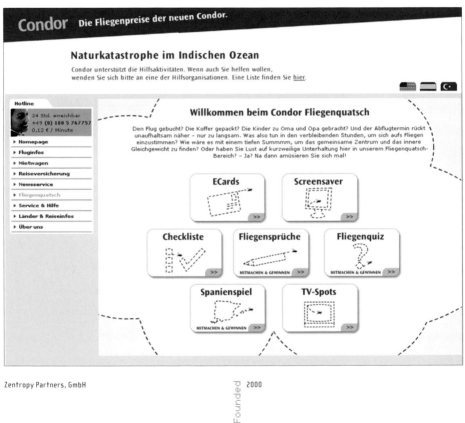

Name — Zentropy Partners, GmbH

Founded — 2000

Team — 1 Creative Director, 1 Group Head Art, 1 Group Head Copy, 2 Copywriters, 5 Art Directors, 2 Motion Graphics Designer, 2 Designer, 11 Application Developers, 4 Content Management, and 5 Project Managers.

Tools — Paper, pencil, and markers.

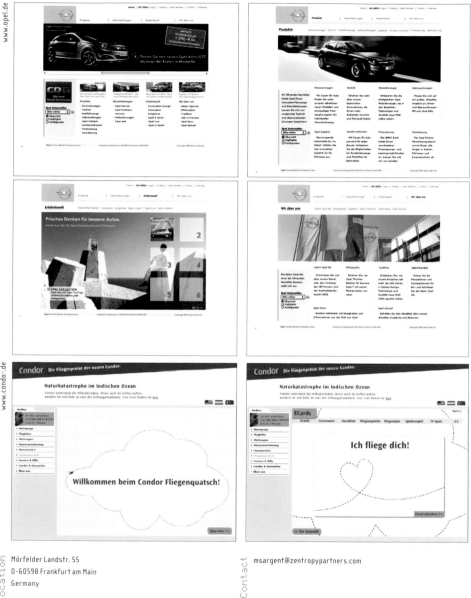

Location

Mörfelder Landstr. 55
D-60598 Frankfurt am Main
Germany

Contact

msargent@zentropypartners.com

Awards

IWPA 2004, best GME site, Opel Best car Configurator in Germany by
Auto Bild, GM CIO Award, IAAA International Automotive Advertising
Awards, Web Awards, International Webpage Awards, etc.

Clients

General Motors, Adam Opel GmbH, Microsoft, Condor,
Mastercard, etc.

ZONAINTERNET

\<BRAZIL\>

www.zonainternet.com

Concept — ZonaInternet Business & Graphic Design tries to offer intelligent solutions of webdesign, prioritising concepts of multidirectional and dynamic navigation, reaching always the highest patterns of layout in perfect harmony with the necessities of our clients. //// ZonaInternet Business & Graphic Design tente de proposer des solutions intelligentes de design Web, en privilégiant les concepts de navigation multidirectionnelle et dynamique, ce qui permet d'atteindre toujours les meilleurs types de layout, en parfaite harmonie avec les nécessités des clients. //// ZonaInternet Business & Graphic Design ist darauf bedacht, intelligente Lösungen für Webdesign zu bieten, mit besonderem Schwerpunkt auf richtungsunabhängiger und dynamischer Navegation, um stets den perfekten Musterentwurf mit den Bedürfnissen unserer Kunden in Einklang zu bringen.

www.vugames.com.br

Name — ZonaInternet Business & Graphic Design

Founded — 2000

Team — 1 Executive Director, 1 Creative Director, 1 New Media Director, 2 Art Directors, 1 Commercial Manager, 1 Flash Designer, 1 Developer, and 1 Office Manager.

Tools — Macromedia Flash, dhtml, XML, etc.

Location

Av. Evandro Lins e Silva 840 conj.1208
Rio de Janeiro - RJ 22631-100
Brasil

Contact

contato@zonainternet.com

Awards

Colunistas Gold Award, Top 10 iBest Award, etc.

Clients

BR, CVRD, Botafogo Praia Shopping, BlueMan, Fernanda Keller,
Furnas Centrais Elétricas, Vivendi Universal Games, Glaxo Smith-
Kline, etc.

CREDITS

TASCHEN is not responsible when web addresses
cannot be reached if they are offline or can be viewed
just with plug-ins.

I would like to thank for all studios and people
involved in the book for their contribution and effort
to provide the materials and information for the book.
Also Daniel for his tireless work contacting all the
offices we wanted to include in this book and for his
work designing and layouting the book.

Animation Now!
Ed. Julius Wiedemann / Flexi-cover, book + DVD, 576 pp. /
€ 29.99/ $ 39.99 / £ 19.99 /
¥ 5.900

Japanese Graphics Now!
Ed. Gisela Kozak, Julius Wiedemann / Flexi-cover,
book + DVD, 608 pp. / € 29.99/
$ 39.99 / £ 19.99 / ¥ 5.900

" ... a celebration of the world's best design. This won't get lost in translation."

—*Sunday Review, Independent on Sunday*, London, on *Japanese Graphics Now!*

"Buy them all and add some pleasure to your life."

African Style
Ed. Angelika Taschen

Alchemy & Mysticism
Alexander Roob

All-American Ads 40s
Ed. Jim Heimann

All-American Ads 50s
Ed. Jim Heimann

All-American Ads 60s
Ed. Jim Heimann

Angels
Gilles Néret

Architecture Now!
Ed. Philip Jodidio

Art Now
Eds. Burkhard Riemschneider, Uta Grosenick

Atget's Paris
Ed. Hans Christian Adam

Berlin Style
Ed. Angelika Taschen

Chairs
Charlotte & Peter Fiell

Christmas
Steven Heller

Design of the 20th Century
Charlotte & Peter Fiell

Design for the 21st Century
Charlotte & Peter Fiell

Devils
Gilles Néret

Digital Beauties
Ed. Julius Wiedemann

Robert Doisneau
Ed. Jean-Claude Gautrand

East German Design
Ralf Ulrich / Photos: Ernst Hedler

Egypt Style
Ed. Angelika Taschen

M.C. Escher

Fashion
Ed. The Kyoto Costume Institute

HR Giger
HR Giger

Grand Tour
Harry Seidler,
Ed. Peter Gössel

Graphic Design
Ed. Charlotte & Peter Fiell

Greece Style
Ed. Angelika Taschen

Halloween Graphics
Steven Heller

Havana Style
Ed. Angelika Taschen

Homo Art
Gilles Néret

Hot Rods
Ed. Coco Shinomiya

Hula
Ed. Jim Heimann

Indian Style
Ed. Angelika Taschen

India Bazaar
Samantha Harrison,
Bari Kumar

Industrial Design
Charlotte & Peter Fiell

Japanese Beauties
Ed. Alex Gross

Krazy Kids' Food
Eds. Steve Roden,
Dan Goodsell

Las Vegas
Ed. Jim Heimann

London Style
Ed. Angelika Taschen

Mexicana
Ed. Jim Heimann

Mexico Style
Ed. Angelika Taschen

Morocco Style
Ed. Angelika Taschen

Extra/Ordinary Objects, Vol. I
Ed. Colors Magazine

Extra/Ordinary Objects, Vol. II
Ed. Colors Magazine

Paris Style
Ed. Angelika Taschen

Penguin
Frans Lanting

20th Century Photography
Museum Ludwig Cologne

Pin-Ups
Ed. Burkhard Riemschneider

Photo Icons I
Hans-Michael Koetzle

Photo Icons II
Hans-Michael Koetzle

Pierre et Gilles
Eric Troncy

Provence Style
Ed. Angelika Taschen

Pussycats
Gilles Néret

Safari Style
Ed. Angelika Taschen

Seaside Style
Ed. Angelika Taschen

Albertus Seba. Butterflies
Irmgard Müsch

Albertus Seba. Shells & Corals
Irmgard Müsch

South African Style
Ed. Angelika Taschen

Starck
Ed Mae Cooper, Pierre Doze,
Elisabeth Laville

Surfing
Ed. Jim Heimann

Sweden Style
Ed. Angelika Taschen

Sydney Style
Ed. Angelika Taschen

Tattoos
Ed. Henk Schiffmacher

Tiffany
Jacob Baal-Teshuva

Tiki Style
Sven Kirsten

Tuscany Style
Ed. Angelika Taschen

Web Design: Best Studios
Ed. Julius Wiedemann

Women Artists
in the 20th and 21st Century
Ed. Uta Grosenick

Web Design: Best Studios

To stay informed about upcoming TASCHEN titles,
please request our magazine at www.taschen.com
or write to TASCHEN, Hohenzollernring 53,
D–50672 Cologne, Germany, Fax: +49-221-254919.
We will be happy to send you a free copy of our magazine
which is filled with information about all of our books.

© 2005 TASCHEN GmbH
Hohenzollernring 53, D-50672 Köln
www.taschen.com

Design: Daniel Siciliano Brêtas
Layout: Daniel Siciliano Brêtas & Julius Wiedemann
Production: Stefan Klatte

Editor: Julius Wiedemann
Assitant-editor: Daniel Siciliano Brêtas
French Translation: Anna Guillerm
German Translation: Heike Lohneis
Spanish Translation: Raquel Valle
Italian Translation: Olivia Papili
Portuguese Translation: Ricardo Esteves Correia

Printed in Italy
ISBN 3-8228-4041-6